Walking in His Footsteps: A Pilgrim's Journey

Dr Andrew C S Koh

Published by Dr Andrew C S Koh Publishing, 2024.

Copyright

© 2025 by Dr Andrew C S Koh

Scan the QR code below to get a free book

Table of Contents

Foreword 1

Preface 3

Testimonials 4

Prologue..5

Chapter 1 | Yardenit Jordan River Baptism Experience 7

Chapter 2 | Reflection on the Mount of Olives 15

Chapter 3 | Temple Mount: A Sacred Space for Three Faiths.......23

Chapter 4 | Enigmatic Mount Carmel 30

Chapter 5 | Tabgha: Miracle of the Loaves and Fishes 36

Chapter 6 | Mount Sinai: Spectacular Sunrise 42

Chapter 7 | Dead Sea: Oasis and Mud Therapy 48

Chapter 8 | Garden Tomb: Spiritual Pilgrimage...................54

Chapter 9 | Petra: A UNESCO Heritage Site 60

Chapter 10 | Galilee: Museum, Boat Ride, and St. Peter's Fish 66

Chapter 11 | Western Wall: Prayer, and Reflection......................74

Chapter 12 | Qumran Caves: Dead Sea Scrolls.......................81

Chapter 13 | Capernaum: Hometown of Jesus 88

Chapter 14 | Magdala: Legacy of Mary Magdalene 96

Chapter 15 | En Gedi: Waterfalls and History in the Judean Desert 101

Chapter 16 | Shiloh: Israel's Ancient Tabernacle Site 108

Chapter 17 | Mount of Beatitudes: Spiritual Retreat 114

Chapter 18 | Church of the Nativity: Birthplace of Jesus........... 120

Chapter 19 | Pool of Bethesda Pool: Healing Power 125

Chapter 20 | Mount Nebo: Bronze Serpent Monument............ 130

Chapter 21 | Hezekiah's Tunnel and Pool of Siloam: Ancient Wonders of Jerusalem 137

Chapter 22 | City of David: Journey Through Biblical History 142

Chapter 23 | Yad Hashmona Biblical Garden: Seder Meal 148

Epilogue.. 153

One Last Thing 154

To my beloved wife, Wai Yin, whose love and unwavering support have been the foundation of everything I do.

To my sons, who have brought joy and purpose into my life.

To my daughters-in-law, who have enriched our family with their warmth and kindness.

To my grandsons and granddaughters, the light of my life, who remind me daily of the beauty and wonder of the world.

To the glory of God, whose grace has guided me through every step of my journey.

To all pilgrims who walk in faith, seeking to follow in His footsteps.

"Whoever claims to live in Him must walk as Jesus did."— 1 John 2:6 (NIV)

Foreword

In Christianity, pilgrimage stands as a powerful symbol of the spiritual journey we embark on. We are all on a journey to connect more deeply with God and discover His purpose for our lives. Dr. Andrew C. S. Koh's book provides a personal and thoughtful account of a pilgrimage, an exploration that transports us from the Holy Land into the sacred landscapes of faith.

Koh offers his insights as a physician and devout Christian, sharing biblical wisdom and personal stories that help readers explore the spiritual journey of traveling in Christ's footsteps.

This book is more than just a travelogue; it serves as a spiritual guide to help us explore and strengthen our faith.

This book inspires those traveling to the Holy Land or seeking a deeper connection with God. Koh's insights help those seeking to deepen their faith and understand God's love and grace better.

I hope this book brings you the same blessings it has given me and reminds everyone to embrace our journey as pilgrims with Christ.

Welcome and best wishes,

Elder David Lim Sui Meng

St. Andrew's Presbyterian Church, Pengkalan, Ipoh, Perak, Malaysia.

July 22, 2025

Preface

This book reflects my deep desire to reconnect with my faith and fully embrace its transformative power. It details my spiritual journey in the Holy Land, where each step resonated with scripture, the presence of Christ, and God's eternal promises.

I invite you to explore these pages as a deep physical and spiritual journey filled with awe, respect, and reflection. Traveling from the ancient hills of Galilee to the sacred streets of Jerusalem, each place I visited was filled with timeless faith. Each pilgrimage transformed my understanding of Scripture and enriched my relationship with God.

I hope to inspire faith as you follow Jesus, whether your journey leads you to faraway places or within yourself. May this path of faith bring you closer to Him, guiding your steps with love and grace.

I wish to thank brother S K Loh for granting me the permission to use many of his photos in this book.

I wish to thank Elder David Lim Sui Meng for writing the forward.

Dr. Andrew C S Koh

July 22, 2025

Testimonials

A deeply personal walk of faith that draws readers closer to Jesus Christ. Honest, heartfelt, and timely, a reminder to walk in His path through life's challenges. Pamela Anne, Barnes & Noble ★★★★★

A refreshing and inspiring journey through the Holy Land, told through the eyes of a devoted follower of Christ. Rowan Creech, Goodreads ★★★★★

An intimate and sacred journey through the Holy Land, capturing the faith and footsteps of the disciples. Beautifully written. Margarita Bailey, Barnes & Noble ★★★★★

A powerful pilgrimage through the sacred sites of Jesus' life, blending history and faith into a moving spiritual experience. Sharmani Jeyaram, Kobo ★★★★★

Dr. Koh masterfully evokes vivid, prayerful moments throughout. The included prayers are thoughtful and beautifully chosen. —Jennifer Surdam, Goodreads ★★★★

Prologue

Those who have embarked on a pilgrimage know that this choice is not made casually. It reflects years of spiritual exploration, a desire to connect with faith, and a deep appreciation for sacred sites that shape its story of salvation. My journey was a long-awaited milestone, both as a Christian and as a writer.

Israel, frequently referred to as the *"Fifth Gospel,"* breathes life into the biblical narratives. Standing in the very places where Christ preached, healed, and sacrificed felt as though time was frozen. My understanding and teachings of Scripture transformed from mere stories into vibrant realities.

My pilgrimage was more than just visiting historical sites; it was about retracing Jesus' footsteps, enhancing my understanding of His mission, and renewing my commitment to follow Him. The Holy Land provided extraordinary experiences that not only offered profound insights but also enriched my relationship with Him.

These pages beckon you to embark on a journey with me. This book chronicles my pilgrimage through the Holy Land, detailing how walking in His footsteps transformed my life. It's meant for those planning their own journey or wanting to learn about these sacred sites.

Chapter 1
Yardenit Jordan River Baptism Experience

Jordan River

The Jordan River Baptismal Site is deeply meaningful for Christian pilgrims. It is the place where Jesus was baptized by John the Baptist. This sacred site gives visitors a chance to think about their faith. They can also join in baptisms in the very waters that hold deep biblical history. Join me as I recount my moving experience at this holy location.

The Jordan River is significant to Christians because it is where John the Baptist baptized Jesus, beginning His public ministry. Pilgrims worldwide visit two well-known baptism sites: Yardenit in Galilee and Bethany Beyond Jordan near the Dead Sea. These sites offer a spiritual link to the events that shaped Christianity, enabling visitors to think deeply on their faith. Many pilgrims choose to join in baptismal ceremonies while there, symbolically renewing their commitment to their beliefs.

A Journey Through History

The journey to the Jordan River transcends mere geography; it is a profound voyage into biblical history. This sacred river flows through the land that God promised to Abraham, his lineage, and the nation of Israel. Joshua led the Israelites from 40 years in the wilderness into their Promised Land (Joshua 3:14-17). The Jordan River appears often throughout the Bible, serving as a powerful symbol of new beginnings and transitions. Notably, it plays a crucial role in the narratives of both Elijah and Elisha. Elijah parted the Jordan's waters, showcasing the divine power given to him and preparing Elisha to take over his role. This river symbolizes faith, miracles, and the enduring covenant between God and His people.

Christians strongly associate the Jordan River with the pivotal moment of Jesus' baptism by John the Baptist. This pivotal event highlights His humility and humanity, demonstrating His sinlessness throughout. Today, pilgrims can visit this sacred river to connect with His life and walk in His footsteps. Many think about the importance of baptism and living a life of faith as they wade through the waters. This transforming experience deepens their spiritual journey and sense of community among believers.

A Holy Atmosphere

As I approached the Jordan River, I was enveloped by a profound sense of reverence. The surrounding landscape exuded serenity, with trees softly rustling in the breeze and the river flowing gently alongside. Despite the crowd, the atmosphere was peaceful, reminding me of important events that happened here 2,000 years ago. I felt the weight of history connecting me to those who came before. It was a moment of reflection and gratitude, igniting a renewed commitment to my own spiritual path.

The river before me was often narrow and murky with sediment. As I stood on its banks, peering into its depths, I was struck by a profound spiritual sensation. At that moment, I recalled the powerful words of John the Baptist: *"I baptize with water for repentance. But after me comes someone more powerful than I, whose sandals I am not worthy to carry. He will baptize you with the Holy Spirit and fire."* (Matthew 3:11). The weight of those words resonated within me, reminding me of the transforming power of faith and purpose. It was as if the river, with all its mysteries and challenges, mirrored the journey of the soul seeking enlightenment.

The Baptismal Experience

Visitors to the Jordan River often take the opportunity to renew their baptism vows. Others choose to get baptized in its holy waters. Participants can select beautiful white robes to wear while singing, praying, and celebrating this special event. I observed a spectrum of emotions, joy, tears, and deep repentance, on the faces of those entering the water. The sunlight reflected off the river, lifting their spirits and highlighting the importance of this sacred moment. Each participant left with not only water but also renewed hope and a commitment to their spiritual journey.

The experience of baptism was a profoundly transforming moment for me. As I entered the cool water and fully submerged myself, I was reminded of Christ's burial, death, and resurrection. Emerging from the water renewed my faith and highlighted baptism as a powerful symbol of my inner change. In that instant, I felt a deep connection to my beliefs and a sense of clarity about my purpose. It felt like the water washed away my doubts. This allowed a stronger, more vibrant faith to flourish within me.

Bethany Beyond the Jordan: The Traditional Baptism Site

Yardenit, near the Sea of Galilee, is a popular site for baptisms. Nonetheless, according to tradition, Jesus was actually immersed in water at Bethany Beyond The Jordan near the Dead Sea. This area is located on Jordan's eastern bank, near an ancient baptismal pool and surrounded by natural desert beauty. It feels more authentic because it lacks commercialization. The serenity of the landscape enhances the spiritual experience, allowing visitors to connect deeply with the history of their faith. I felt a deep sense of peace and belonging, as if the spirit of those before me was still here.

Bethany Beyond the Jordan features archaeological remains from the early Christian era, offering visitors a rich historical and reflective experience. Believed to be the site of Jesus' baptism, it exudes an ambiance of ancient reverence that captivates all who visit. Each step through the site reveals stories etched into the stones, inviting personal reflections on faith and heritage. This link to a key event in Christian history highlights Bethany's importance as a pilgrimage site.

Spiritual Impact

This journey is a deeply spiritual pilgrimage. For centuries, individuals have flocked to this sacred site to meet the divine in a profound way. Baptism transcends mere ritual; it marks the beginning of a lifelong journey of transformation and renewal. As pilgrims immerse themselves in the waters, they become renewed, carrying their experiences and new commitments with them. Each splash resonates with echoes of hope, faith, and a promise of a brighter path ahead.

I stood by the Jordan River. I felt a strong connection to its history. Many believers were baptized here before me. This experience illuminated the understanding that my faith is a journey, and baptism is a significant milestone within that journey. It served as a reminder of the continuous growth and evolution of one's beliefs. Each step reminded me to embrace the changes that faith brings, leading to a better understanding of purpose and community.

Practical Information for Visitors

Yardenit is by the calm Sea of Galilee. Bethany Beyond the Jordan is easily reached from Amman or the Allenby Bridge. Both sites offer a serene atmosphere where visitors can ponder on their own spiritual journeys. These locations offer a deep connection to the foundations of faith, whether for reflection or baptism.

The ideal time to visit Bethany is during the spring and fall, as summers can be excessively hot. Both locations offer the choice to rent or buy baptismal robes. Visitors planning to be baptized should bring extra clothing and towels. Additionally, it's advisable to arrive early to fully partake in the peaceful surroundings and engage in personal reflection. This ensures a more meaningful experience as you prepare for the sacred ceremony.

Tip:

Enhance your visit by bringing a Bible to read and contemplate the profound significance of Jesus' baptism in Christianity. Opting for a guided tour can further enrich your experience with valuable historical and biblical insights. Take time to connect with fellow visitors while you explore the history and teachings. Sharing thoughts and experiences can deepen your understanding and appreciation of the occasion.

A Pilgrimage to Remember

The Yardenit Jordan River Baptismal Site offered a profoundly spiritual experience that I will cherish. My visit was not only about history. It made me think about my past and current faith journeys. It also opened up new opportunities for my relationship with faith. Yardenit is a special place for baptism and a deeper understanding of God's grace. As I stood by the water's edge, I felt connected to the generations of believers. They had come before me. This sacred site deepened my faith. It prompted me to consider on how to apply those teachings in my daily life.

As I left, I remembered the words from God, the Father to Jesus during His baptism. He said, *"This is my Son, whom I love; with Him, I am well pleased"* (Matthew 3:17). These words reminded me that I am a valued child of God, meant to live with love, humility, and grace. Embracing this identity encourages me to extend kindness and compassion to others, just as I have received it. Each day presents a chance to embody these teachings, fostering a sense of community and connection with those around me.

In moments of doubt, I find strength in remembering that my worth is rooted in His unwavering love. This motivates me to positively impact others and encourages my commitment to serve with kindness. As I embrace this calling, I strive to be a beacon of hope and light in their lives. This helps me affirm my identity and encourages others to see their worth as cherished children of God. Through this journey, I recognize the power of vulnerability and the importance of sharing our stories. By doing so, we create a space where others feel safe to explore their own paths of healing and growth.

Grace

Grace, like a river, soft and still,Flows through the valleys, bends to my will.Unseen, yet felt in the depths of my soul.A love that heals, a peace that makes whole.

Grace in the morning, new like the dawn,Washing away the burdens long drawn.It whispers hope when all feels lost,A gift unearned, no matter the cost.

In moments of weakness, it gently appears,Wiping away the stains of my fears.It lifts me high when I am low,Grace, my refuge, in its light I grow.

Not by my works, not by my might, But grace alone, through darkest night.It finds me broken, and calls me by name,Grace unending, forever the same.

Through every trial, every storm's embrace,I stand in awe of this wondrous grace.A gift so pure, so freely given,Grace is the path that leads to heaven.

www.drandrewcskoh.com/poems

Chapter 2

Reflection on the Mount of Olives

Mount of Olives

My journey to the Mount of Olives was an exploration into Christian history. Standing where Jesus prayed and then rose up into heaven was truly spiritually fulfilling for me. Reflecting upon its significance within both scripture and Christian tradition was equally profound. Join me as I ponder upon this profound pilgrimage site!

The Mount of Olives stands as one of Christianity's most esteemed sites, a location steeped in biblical history. As I approached this sacred mountain, located to the east of Jerusalem's Old City, a sense of awe enveloped me. The Mount of Olives is renowned for its stunning panoramic views of Jerusalem. It also holds profound significance in the context of Jesus Christ's life and ministry.

The ancient olive trees that dot the landscape whisper stories of the past. They remind visitors of the moments when Jesus found solace and strength in prayer. Every step I took felt like treading on holy ground. I immersed myself in the rich tapestry of faith and history. This sacred place embodies these aspects.

As I stood there, I realized that countless pilgrims before me had felt the same sense of reverence. They experienced a profound connection. The air was still and seemed to invite reflection. It urged me to contemplate my own journey of faith in the shadow of such an iconic landmark.

Historical and Biblical Significance

The Mount of Olives has been pivotal in a multitude of significant biblical events throughout its extensive history. Often referenced in Scripture, especially in the New Testament, this holy ground saw many crucial moments. This is where Jesus mourned for Jerusalem (Luke 19:41-44). Here, He delivered His prophetic Olivet Discourse (Matthew 24-25). He prayed in the Garden of Gethsemane. Jesus ultimately ascended into heaven after His resurrection (Acts 1:9-12).

Each of these events shaped the course of spiritual history. They also deepened the connection between the earthly and the divine. Standing there, I could almost hear the echoes of prayers and teachings. These sounds have resonated through the ages. They invited me to explore the depths of my own beliefs.

As I wandered along the pathways, I couldn't help but envision Jesus and His disciples walking these same grounds. Their hearts were filled with anticipation for what was to come. Standing atop the Mount of Olives brought the Bible to life in a way I did not experience before. It made its rich history feel incredibly tangible.

Jerusalem looked breathtaking from this vantage point. It was a tapestry of ancient stone and modern life. Both are interwoven in a sacred narrative. Time seemed to stand still. This allowed me to ponder the profound significance of faith. I reflected on its ability to transcend generations.

The time I spent in the Garden of Gethsemane was a profound highlight of my visit. It is nestled at the base of the Mount of Olives. This sacred site is thought to be where Jesus prayed before His betrayal and arrest. Within its ancient walls, the remarkable olive trees stood for nearly 2,000 years. They bear silent witness to that pivotal night in Jesus' life. These trees add a haunting depth to this holy place.

While in the garden, I reflected on Jesus' profound anguish. I considered His ultimate surrender to His Father's will. His reflection showed His boundless love for humanity. Praying in the same garden where He sought refuge before His crucifixion was deeply humbling. It was a moving experience.

As I knelt beneath the gnarled branches, I felt a sense of connection that transcended time. It was a reminder of the struggles we all face. The peacefulness of the garden enveloped me, offering solace and hope in the midst of life's challenges.

A Place of Worship and Reflection

Beyond its rich biblical history, the Mount of Olives is home to several significant Christian landmarks. These include the Church of Pater Noster, where Jesus imparted the Lord's Prayer. The Chapel of Ascension marks the spot where Christ ascended to heaven. Each of these sacred sites offered me profound moments for reflection and prayer, profoundly enriching my spiritual journey.

The atmosphere was thick with reverence. As I walked among these holy grounds, I felt increasingly aware of the countless souls who had come before me. They sought guidance and peace. Every prayer uttered within these walls seemed to echo through the ages, bridging the gap between believers past and current.

During my visit to the Church of All Nations, I was captivated by its breathtaking architecture. This place is also referred to as the Basilica of the Agony. Its reverent ambiance left a strong impression on me. The interior is right where Jesus prayed in Gethsemane. It boasts remarkable mosaics that portray scenes from His Passion. This serene environment provided the perfect backdrop for meditation as I reflected on His profound sacrifice.

The fragrance of the olive trees surrounded me. I closed my eyes. I allowed the weight of my thoughts to drift away. At that moment, I felt a deep connection to my faith. The stories of those who had prayed here before enveloped me in a warm embrace.

At the peak of the Mount of Olives, I was greeted by a breathtaking panorama of Jerusalem's Old City. The golden Dome of the Rock glimmered in the sunlight. It invited me to think about the rich tapestry of history, faith, and tradition. This tapestry weaves through this remarkable city.

I gazed upon the ancient walls and the bustling streets below, I felt a sense of gratitude. The spiritual journey had brought me to this sacred place. Each stone seemed to whisper the tales of devotion and resilience. These tales echoed through the ages. They inspired me to deepen my own commitment.

I was moved by the poignant image of Jesus weeping for Jerusalem, longing for its people to return to God. At that moment of reflection, I realized that the Mount of Olives embodies both profound sorrow and remarkable hope.

The air was thick with a sense of yearning. It seemed as if the essence of the city held onto the prayers of countless generations. In that sacred space, my heart felt intertwined with the collective longing for peace. This connection drew me closer to the divine presence that permeated the atmosphere.

Personal Reflection

My visit to the Mount of Olives was a profound blend of history and spirituality. This site is steeped in biblical significance. It is enveloped in a serene atmosphere. It offered me a chance to pause and contemplate deeply on my faith and relationship with God. The timeless teachings of Jesus and His boundless love stirred a wealth of cherished memories within me!

As I stood amid the ancient trees, I could almost hear the echoes of His words in my soul. They urged me to embrace compassion. They urged me to embrace forgiveness. This experience fortified my faith.

It also ignited a renewed commitment to carry those lessons into my everyday life.

This journey was an emotional pilgrimage. It was an opportunity to reconnect with my spiritual roots. I had a chance to ponder on the life and ministry of Jesus. It helped rejuvenate my spiritual path. The Mount of Olives serves as a timeless beacon of hope in Christ. It embodies both sorrow and joy. I await His return, just as His disciples did after His ascension.

In moments of quiet reflection, I could sense the presence of those who walked alongside Him. They reminded me of the strength that comes from unity in faith. As I left the sacred site, I felt an invigorating sense of purpose. I was ready to share the light of Christ's teachings with the world around me.

Conclusion

Visiting the Mount of Olives was a transforming experience that enriched my understanding and admiration for Jesus' life and ministry. This revered mountain is steeped in biblical history and spiritual significance for every Christian pilgrim.

As I departed, I carried with me a revitalized sense of purpose. My faith and hope were renewed. I felt deeply grateful for the opportunity to walk in the footsteps of Jesus. I contemplated His timeless love and grace.

My journey there was not just a physical trek but a profound spiritual awakening that resonated within my soul. I realized that each step on that sacred ground showed the enduring legacy of faith. This legacy binds us all together.

The Mount of Olives in Jerusalem is an essential pilgrimage destination for Christian travelers and spiritual seekers. It is important along with the Garden of Gethsemane and the site of Jesus' ascension. These iconic biblical sites are essential to religious tourism in the Holy Land. They are also integral to the historic Old City of Jerusalem.

My journey to the Mount of Olives was profoundly transforming. It offered a profound connection to the life and ministry of Jesus. The sacred mountain encompasses the serene Garden of Gethsemane. It also includes the revered Church of the Ascension. This mountain is filled with rich biblical history and deep spiritual meaning.

I stood there, surrounded by peace. I couldn't help but feel the weight of centuries of prayer and devotion in the air. Each moment spent at these sites reaffirmed my faith. It deepened my understanding of the spiritual journey that countless others have undertaken before me.

CHURCH OF ALL NATIONS OR BASILICA OF THE AGONY IS A ROMAN CATHOLIC CHURCH ADJACENT TO THE GARDEN OF GETHSEMANE. WE WERE VERY FORTUNATE TO BE ABLE TO TOUCH THE SECTION OF BEDROCK WHERE JESUS IS BELIEVED TO HAVE PRAYED BEFORE HIS ARREST.

Everyday is a blessing

Chapter 3

Temple Mount: A Sacred Space for Three Faiths

Temple Mount

My visit to the Temple Mount was an extraordinary foray into both biblical history and modern-day spirituality. I stood on the site of Solomon's Temple. I felt the weight of centuries of religious devotion. The place carries profound spiritual significance. Join me as I explore its importance in Jewish tradition. Then I will examine its significance in Christian belief and Muslim customs. Finally, I will share my personal reflections on this pivotal pilgrimage experience.

Jerusalem's Old City

The Temple Mount in Jerusalem's Old City is one of the most revered and contested religious sites in the world. It is cherished by Jews, Christians, and Muslims alike as a convergence of faith. It signifies history, tradition, and worship. My visit to this sacred landmark was not merely a physical journey. It became a profound spiritual pilgrimage. This journey linked me to millennia of devotion and worship.

Each step on the ancient stones felt like walking through layers of history. It was as if I could hear the whispers of prayers offered long ago. This connection ignited a deep sense of belonging. I realized how intertwined our faiths truly are, even though divisions often separate us.

I stood in the shadows of past glories. The weight of each faith's narrative washed over me. This reminded me of the shared roots from which they flourished. It was a powerful moment of unity. It urged me to think about the need for understanding and compassion in our modern world.

In this sacred space, I found a place of worship. It was also a beacon of hope for harmony among diverse beliefs. The experience left an indelible mark on my heart. It inspires me to carry its message of peace into my everyday life.

Historical and Religious Significance

The Temple Mount is a cornerstone of Jewish history. It is renowned as the site of Solomon's Temple, or the First Temple. This temple was built in the 10th century BCE. The Babylonians ultimately destroyed it. It was later rebuilt after the exile. The Romans obliterated it in 70 CE. These temples were more than mere structures. They were the spiritual and cultural epicenters of ancient Israel. Worshipers gathered there to connect directly with God.

Christians hold the Temple Mount in high regard for its profound Jewish heritage. They also value its significant connections to the New Testament. Jesus imparted his teachings within the courts of the Second Temple. He famously cleared it of money changers who had corrupted its sanctity (Matthew 21:12-13). Today, this sacred site serves as a vital space for spiritual reflection and a poignant reminder of Jesus' ministry.

Islam designates the Temple Mount as Haram al-Sharif. This means "Noble Sanctuary." It houses both the stunning Dome of the Rock and the revered Al-Aqsa Mosque. This sacred site is believed by some Muslims to be the location of Prophet Muhammad's Night Journey to heaven. The majestic golden Dome of the Rock stands out against Jerusalem's skyline. It symbolizes the city's profound religious heritage.

Walking Through History

As I set foot on the Temple Mount, I was overwhelmed by the profound historical significance that enveloped the site. This vast, elevated platform, surrounded by ancient walls, has borne witness to centuries of faith, conflict, and devotion. The original Jewish temples have long since vanished. Yet, enduring remnants like the Western Wall stand as powerful testaments to their lasting legacy.

The Temple Mount area is a remarkable archaeological gem. It showcases ancient stones, pathways, and staircases. These elements vividly narrate its rich and vibrant history. As I explored these captivating spaces, I envisioned pilgrims arriving in waves. They came from the time of Solomon through the era of Roman rule. They sought to offer their sacrifices and prayers at this historic site.

Standing before the Western Wall was a deeply moving experience during my visit. It is the nearest point for Jews to the original site of the Holy of Holies in the temple. The wall lies outside the Temple Mount itself. Yet, it serves as a powerful emblem of their enduring bond to this sacred space.

The sheer weight of history reverberated through the air. I watched people of all backgrounds leave handwritten prayers. They tucked these prayers into its crevices. It was a poignant reminder of the unbroken connection between past and present. Faith and hope converge in a space that transcends time.

At this moment, I felt a profound sense of solidarity with those who had come before me. Each prayer was a whisper of devotion that echoed through the ages. It was a beautiful testament to the resilience of faith. It celebrated the human spirit and yearning that knows no boundaries.

Dome of the Rock and Al-Aqsa Mosque

Temple Mount holds a rich Jewish and Christian history embedded in its very foundations. Yer, today it is primarily recognized for two of Islam's holiest sites: the Dome of the Rock and Al-Aqsa Mosque. These magnificent structures symbolize the sacredness of Islam. The Dome is traditionally linked to a pivotal moment in Jewish and Christian beliefs. Here, Abraham prepared to sacrifice Isaac according to Jewish and Christian traditions. Alternatively, it was linked to Ishmael according to Islamic tradition.

The Al-Aqsa Mosque, located nearby, is a vibrant center of worship and spiritual practice. While non-Muslims are restricted from entering the mosque, I found great joy in appreciating its stunning beauty from the outside. These remarkable structures stand as powerful symbols of the diverse religions that coexist on the Temple Mount.

Reflection on Faith and Unity

My visit to the Temple Mount provided a profound history lesson. It also offered a chance for deep reflection on faith and unity. In this single location, three major religions converge. Each religion declares it sacred. The weight of history profoundly impacts contemporary life.

While wandering through the open courtyards, I raised prayers for peace and unity among those who hold this space dear. I felt a profound connection to all who had sought God before me. These were individuals seeking through prayer or devotion. They could be Jewish, Christian, or Muslim.

The air was thick with a sense of reverence. Each step resonated with the echoes of countless footsteps across millennia. It reminded me that despite our differences, we share a common yearning for solace. We all long for understanding and harmony in a world often marked by division.

As I stood in the midst of this sacred convergence, I felt the enduring power of faith. It bridges gaps and ignites hope. The vibrant tapestry of beliefs intertwined in this space. It served as a testament to humanity's quest for connection and love amid the chaos of existence.

Personal Pilgrimage

The Temple Mount visit was a profound moment in my Christian pilgrimage to the Holy Land. Standing on that sacred ground was deeply moving. It poignantly underscored the significance of Israel in Jesus's life. It also highlighted the enduring presence of God in my life.

This visit reinforced my belief. Temples and structures may rise and fall. Yet, the true sanctuary of God dwells within each person's heart. The Temple Mount is a powerful symbol of faith's enduring strength. It also signifies humanity's deep wish to connect with the divine.

I gazed at the ancient stones that had borne witness to countless prayers and hopes. I felt an overwhelming sense of gratitude for the shared history that binds us all. It was a reminder that, regardless of our differences, we are united in our search for meaning and the sacred.

At that moment, I realized the importance of cherishing these connections to my past as I navigate my spiritual journeys. Every step on that holy ground brought me nearer to understanding profound love. This love and grace transcend all cultural divides.

Conclusion

Visiting the Temple Mount was an extraordinary voyage through history and spirituality. This revered site was once home to King Solomon's Temple. Now, it is adorned with the magnificent Al-Aqsa Mosque and the iconic Dome of the Rock. It offers a unique chance to contemplate its deep spiritual significance. This significance binds three of the world's major religions. The Temple Mount is filled with reverence and peace. It is a place of prayer. It is an indispensable destination for any Christian pilgrimage to the Holy Land.

I stood there, immersed in the atmosphere of devotion. It enveloped the sacred space. I felt a profound sense of belonging to something much greater than myself. History and belief echoed within me. They reminded me that these spiritual ties shape my present. They guide my path forward.

The experience left an indelible mark on my soul. It urged me to think about the shared threads of faith. These threads connect diverse communities across the globe. It was a reminder that, despite our different beliefs, we all contribute to a larger narrative. This narrative transcends time and nurtures our shared humanity.

Chapter 4
Enigmatic Mount Carmel

Mount Carmel

A visit to Mount Carmel transcends breathtaking vistas; it is an immersive journey through biblical history and spiritual introspection. Explore the rich legacy of this sacred mountain. This is where Elijah famously challenged the prophets of Baal. All of this happens while surrounded by the awe-inspiring landscapes that define this historic site in Israel.

Introduction

Mount Carmel in northern Israel is steeped in profound religious and spiritual significance, intertwining both biblical history and contemporary spirituality. As I got closer, my excitement grew. I knew I was nearing the legendary site where Elijah confronted the prophets of Baal. The amazing views from the summit heightened my excitement, revealing a landscape rich with history. Every step I took felt like a journey through time, connecting me to sacred events of the past.

The air felt reverent as I observed my surroundings, thinking of the many pilgrims who walked this path before me. The mountain seemed to whisper secrets of faith and resilience, prompting me to think about my spiritual journey. I paused. I felt the weight of history around me. I breathed in the scent of sagebrush and crisp mountain air. At that moment, I felt a deep sense of belonging. It was as if those who fought for their beliefs were guiding me forward.

A Biblical Landmark

Mount Carmel holds a prestigious place in biblical history, particularly in the Old Testament. In 1 Kings 18, the Prophet Elijah courageously challenged King Ahab and the prophets of Baal. He demonstrated God's great power in a memorable confrontation. This event still inspires believers today. Standing where Elijah once stood gave me a powerful connection to this significant biblical story, making the experience unforgettable.

As I gazed at the landscape, I could almost hear the echoes of the ancient battle. The prayers of the faithful seemed to transcend through time. This sacred site symbolized the ongoing struggle between faith and doubt, which deeply resonated with my own journey. The winds seemed to carry whispers of hope and redemption, reminding me of the importance of standing firm in belief.

Each moment on that sacred ground reminded us that faith can overcome even the darkest times. As the sun set, a golden light spread over the hills, and I felt a deep sense of peace. The essence of the place reassured me. I was not alone in my struggles. In the quiet twilight, the lines between past and present blurred, helping me think on the lessons I've learned.

I knew, then, that every challenge had shaped me, paving the path to resilience and understanding. With each breath of the cool evening air, I felt my worries lifting. They were replaced by hope and peace. This sanctuary had become a testament to the power of perseverance in the face of adversity.

Carmelite Monastery

Mount Carmel boasts a remarkable history that transcends biblical times, having been home to diverse cultures since antiquity. The summit provides breathtaking views of the Jezreel Plain, highlighting the area's strategic and spiritual significance. During my visit, I also explored the Carmelite Monastery, which commemorates Elijah's victory and devotion to God.

The tranquil environment of the monastery created an ideal setting for contemplation amid the beauty of nature. Sitting in silence, I felt connected to the generations who had walked these paths. Each generation left their mark on this sacred land. The whispers of history lingered in the air, inviting me to ponder on my own journey of faith and purpose.

As the sun set and cast golden hues, I recognized the importance of embracing solitude. This experience enhanced my knowledge of the land's history and my spiritual journey. In this calm atmosphere, I gained clarity amid my chaotic thoughts and learned to appreciate the present moment. Moments of stillness are crucial for nurturing the soul and gaining a deeper understanding of life.

Summit of Mount Carmel

Reaching the summit of Mount Carmel was an unforgettable experience. From here, you can see stunning views of the Mediterranean Sea, and on clear days, Mount Hermon is also visible! This part of my journey was truly remarkable. The rich history and beautiful landscapes made it so. Each view reflected the area's past.

At the summit, I felt deeply connected to the land and its stories. It was as if the whispers of ancient travelers filled the breeze. This stunning view enhanced my appreciation for the many generations that shaped the world I experienced. Standing there, I reflected on my journey and the experiences that brought me to this moment. The peaceful surroundings made me ponder the connection between nature and history, filling me with respect for both.

As I pondered these thoughts, the sun began to dip below the horizon, casting a warm glow over the landscape. At that moment, I realized that every journey is shaped by my experiences. Each thread holds stories of triumph and struggle, binding me to those who came before me. As the light faded, I felt a renewed sense of purpose and gratitude for the journey ahead.

Spiritual Reflection

My visit to Mount Carmel transcended mere history; it became a deeply spiritual experience. Standing where Elijah called down fire from heaven deepened my understanding of the scriptures. This moment inspired deep reflection on faith during difficult times, akin to Elijah's example.

I closed my eyes. I felt a sense of unity with those who had stood in this sacred place before me. The whispers of history guided my thoughts, reminding me that faith often shines brightest in the face of adversity. In that stillness, I found strength in the assurance that challenges can lead to profound growth.

The majestic beauty of the landscape surrounding Mount Carmel became a symbol of the resilience of the human spirit. With each breath of the crisp mountain air, I felt rejuvenated and emboldened to confront my own trials. This connection to the past deepened my understanding of faith. It inspired me to face the future with courage and hope.

Spiritual Significance

Mount Carmel holds profound significance for Christians, Jews, and Muslims, representing a cultural and religious crossroads. The Carmelite Order, founded in the 12th century, reflects a strong devotion to God, inspired by the prophet Elijah. This enduring legacy has shaped the spiritual practices and traditions of these faiths, intertwining their histories in a unique tapestry.

I walked the ancient paths. I felt a strong sense of unity among the various beliefs that have thrived in this sacred space. Standing among the tall trees and gentle winds, I felt a calming peace that highlighted our shared values. This experience illuminated how, despite our differences, we can find common ground in our quest for meaning and transcendence.

It was a reminder that spirituality often transcends the boundaries of individual doctrines. In those moments of reflection, the essence of compassion and understanding emerged as the true heart of our journeys. I noticed that moments of quiet reflection can bring people together and strengthen connections. In this shared space, it became clear that our spiritual journeys may vary. Yet, we all share a common goal of love and empathy for each other.

Conclusion

My journey to Mount Carmel deepened my faith and enriched my understanding of its profound historical and spiritual significance. Mount Carmel offers a profound connection between biblical history and modern life. This experience is available to everyone, no matter their religious background or cultural interest. The visit is truly rewarding. Walking the paths of prophets is breathtaking. Experiencing the divine wonders of this sacred place is also awe-inspiring!

Surrounded by nature's beauty and history, I felt a renewed sense of purpose and belonging. Leaving Mount Carmel, I took with me a promise to promote love and understanding in my everyday life. This promise ignited my commitment to share the lessons learned during my visit.

Embracing the spirit of Mount Carmel, I strive to inspire others to seek their own journeys of faith and discovery. Reflecting on my experiences, I see how our stories are interconnected, creating a shared tapestry of hope and inspiration. It is my wish to encourage meaningful conversations that bridge gaps and foster unity among all who seek the light.

Chapter 5
Tabgha: Miracle of the Loaves and Fishes

Tabgha

Explore Tabgha, the sacred site where Jesus famously performed the miracle of multiplying loaves and fish. Experience its spiritual significance, tranquil atmosphere, and rich historical landmarks that make this holy destination a must-visit!

Tabgha is a serene sanctuary nestled by the Sea of Galilee, rich in deep biblical heritage. Jesus performed a miraculous event in Tabgha. He fed more than 5,000 people with just five loaves and two fishes. Thus, Tabgha serves as a tranquil oasis for reflection. It holds profound spiritual significance for both pilgrims and travelers.

Tabgha is located on the northwestern shore of the Sea of Galilee in Israel. It stands out as a pivotal Christian pilgrimage destination. It is known as the site where Jesus fed more than 5,000 people with five loaves and two fish. The site draws pilgrims seeking deep spiritual experiences linked to Christ's ministry. On my pilgrimage, I connected deeply with this serene and sacred site.

The lush landscapes and tranquil waters create an atmosphere perfect for contemplation and prayer. As I walked the grounds, I felt a sense of connection to the countless pilgrims who had come before me. Each one embraced the profound legacy of faith that permeates Tabgha.

The vibrant colors of nature highlighted the miracles of the past. They reminded me of the simplicity and strength of Jesus's teachings. I felt grateful with each step for the chance to experience such an important moment in history and spirituality.

Historical and Biblical Significance

Tabgha is profoundly linked with a celebrated miracle in all the four Gospels. This miracle is the Multiplication of Loaves and Fishes. Here Jesus multiplied a small meal to feed an immense crowd. Tabgha (also referred to as Heptapegon in Greek), means seven springs. Here is where the Lord Jesus performed His greatest miracle as described by the four Gospel writers.

The serene landscape of Tabgha, with its seven springs, provided a perfect backdrop for reflection on such a miraculous event. I could picture the crowd gathered to witness a powerful show of compassion and generosity. As the people awaited a sign, their hopes were high, and their faith palpable.

This setting deepens historical significance and highlights the lasting impact of faith and community. In this sacred place, five loaves and two fish were miraculously transformed to feed thousands. The miracle reminds us of the power of sharing and how small acts of kindness can lead to divine provision.

Church of Multiplication

Tabgha is home to one of its most astonishing attractions: the Church of the Multiplication. This beautiful edifice, which stands on the foundations of earlier Byzantine churches, was completed in 1982. At its center is a colorful mosaic of two fish and loaves. This artwork celebrates the miraculous event that happened at this sacred site.

Visitors are touched by artwork illustrating the miracle, prompting reflections on the value of generosity and community. The serene atmosphere invites prayer and contemplation, allowing one to connect deeply with the history and spirituality of the place. Inside the church is an altar. Underneath this is a stone believed to be the spot where Christ sat during the miracle of the feeding.

My Experience in Tabgha

Upon arriving in Tabgha, I was enveloped by a sense of tranquility. The mesmerizing turquoise waters of the Sea of Galilee, framed by distant mountains, created a breathtaking backdrop. As I walked through the pathways and gardens, I felt transported back in time. I reflected on the remarkable events that occurred here over two thousand years ago.

My visit was highlighted by entering the Church of the Multiplication. Standing before the ancient mosaic floor near the altar was unforgettable, making me feel connected to this remarkable miracle. The mosaic's design, depicting two fishes and a basket full of bread, spoke volumes about faith and God's provision.

Sitting by the Sea of Galilee, near the church, I enjoyed the soothing sound of waves gently hitting the rocks. This peaceful place encouraged reflection and prayer. It brought back memories of the crowds that once came here for one of Jesus's remarkable miracles.

I took in the tranquil beauty around me. I imagined the joy and hope that filled the hearts of those present during that miraculous event. It was a moment that connected me to the past and renewed my faith and purpose.

Spiritual Reflection

The tranquil atmosphere of Tabgha evokes profound contemplation. While exploring this sacred space, I reflected on the importance of the miracle of the loaves and fishes. It embodies a powerful message about God's provision for both our physical and spiritual needs, beautifully encouraging generosity. A single small gift in Jesus' hands can create a tremendous impact, illustrating the abundance of His grace and care!

For Christian pilgrims, Tabgha represents more than just a historical site; it is a profound opportunity to strengthen their faith. My visit provided me with a deeper connection to Jesus' teachings on faith, hope, and trust in God's divine plan. In this peaceful spot, I felt a wave of calm, recalling how faith had guided me through tough times. This experience enhanced my understanding and sparked a desire to share the lessons of love and abundance with others.

Other Attractions

In addition to the Church of the Multiplication, there are several other significant sites worth exploring in Tabgha:

The Church of the Primacy of Saint Peter:

This historic church is a tribute. It commemorates when Jesus appeared to His disciples after His resurrection in John chapter 21. In this event, He gave Peter a leadership role. The peaceful atmosphere of the Church of the Primacy enhances the spiritual experience. It encourages visitors to contemplate the significance of leadership and service in their lives. The beautiful Sea of Galilee provides a breathtaking backdrop for pilgrims to ponder on their faith amid nature's beauty.

Sea of Galilee

A boat ride across the Sea of Galilee helps visitors appreciate its history. It includes stories like Jesus walking on water and calming storms. The gentle waves against the boat evoke the presence of biblical stories that took place on these shores. This peaceful journey provides a chance to ponder and connect with teachings of love and faith while exploring history.

Conclusion

My journey to Tabgha was profound and spiritually enriching. It was unforgettable. It allowed me to witness one of the most renowned miracles in Christianity. The tranquil atmosphere and rich sense of sacred history make Tabgha an exceptional pilgrimage site. Whether for religious reasons or to explore ancient Israeli history, your experience will be remarkable!

Departing from Tabgha, I was filled with a renewed sense of faith and gratitude. The story of Jesus feeding five thousand with loaves and fish reminds us of His provision. His abundance is still available in our lives today. This experience has deepened my understanding of faith and the profound connections between history and spirituality. As I left, I took with me memories of the beautiful landscapes. I also carried with me a reminder of the miracles that inspire many believers.

Humility

Humility, a quiet grace,Unseen, yet bright in every place.It bows its head, it yields the floor, Seeking no praise, yet offering more.

It whispers soft, not loud or proud,Unmoved by cheers or boasting's crowd.In strength, it kneels; in power, it's still,A heart that's bent to God's good will.

It doesn' t boast or seek the throne,It lifts the weak, it stands alone.With gentle hands, it serves the least,And at the lowest, finds its feast.

For in humility, love is found,Its roots grow deep in solid ground. It rises not, but lifts the soul, Giving life, making whole.

It knows that all is not its own, But grace received from God alone.In every act, in every breath,Humility walks the path of death.

www.drandrewcskoh.com/poems

Chapter 6
Mount Sinai: Spectacular Sunrise

Mount Sinai

Mount Sinai is also known as Jabal Musa and is located in the Sinai Peninsula, Egypt. This is one of many locations that claim to be the biblical Mount Sinai. According to the Bible, Torah and Quran, this is where Moses received the Ten Commandments. Standing at 2,285 meters high, this mountain range is surrounded on all four sides by even higher peaks.

Mount Sinai is located in the Sinai Peninsula of Egypt on the eastern side of the Gulf of Suez. The breathtaking views from the summit reveal an awe-inspiring landscape that stretches far into the horizon. As the sun rises, dawn's vibrant colors brighten the rugged landscape, creating a captivating atmosphere for visitors.

Checking in

I was so fortunate to be able to climb Mount Sinai in Egypt with other travelers many years ago. We arrived at the base of Mount Sinai at 7pm. After checking into our hotel, we had dinner and went to bed early to prepare for the climb. The excitement built as we set our alarms for an early start, eager to catch the sunrise from the peak. We had no idea that the journey would test us physically and emotionally, making the reward even more remarkable.

Debrief

Our hearts were pounding with anticipation as we eagerly anticipated the journey ahead. At 1 am, the guide gave us a briefing on the ascent. They then taught us how to ride a camel. After some initial awkwardness and laughter, we managed to find our balance and began to feel more confident. Riding through the quiet desert under the stars was a magical experience, filled with the awe for the surrounding beauty.

Camel Ride

We began our climb at 2 am. The first leg of the journey was done on camelback, which added an extra element of adventure and discovery. It was an incredible experience that increased my sense of exploration.

I heard occasional sounds as I carefully led my camel along the rough, winding, and dark paths. I looked up into the Middle Eastern night sky and saw the stars. Their brilliance seemed to echo the excitement I felt within. With each step, I could feel the anticipation building for what lay ahead in the early morning light.

Abraham

I embarked on a journey back in time through the intricate tunnel of my mind. In the depths of my imagination, I can vividly envision God speaking to Abraham. He promised him that his descendants would multiply like the countless stars scattered across the enchanting Middle Eastern night sky. This vision takes place more than 4000 years ago. I was amazed by the historical significance of this mountain as we climbed to the summit.

We arrived at the station after a long and exhilarating camel ride. We dismounted the camel here, and started climbing uphill, navigating the steep terrain. Our ascent began as the darkness gave way to dawn. The first light of day cast a golden hue over the landscape, revealing the rugged beauty that surrounded us. Every step felt adventurous, revealing secrets in the mountain's ancient rocks.

Spectacular Sunrise

We arrived at the peak of Mount Sinai at 5am and began to wait for sunrise. As we waited, the sky gradually brightened and more landscape features became visible. When the sun finally rose, it painted the skies in stunning shades of orange and pink. It was absolutely magnificent.

The sun's warm glow cast a golden light on the rugged terrain, creating a stunning landscape. Standing there, we felt a deep sense of connection to nature and the history that surrounded us. It was as if the land itself was awakening, revealing secrets hidden in the shadows of the night. Each moment felt sacred, a reminder of the beauty and power of the world we inhabit.

The Descend

At 6 am, we began our descent. Mount Sinai's rock terrain was revealed in the dawn light, which contrasted starkly with the darkness of the night. We enjoyed the peaceful atmosphere and views as we slowly descended.

Our journey ended at St. Catherine's Monastery, an ancient, revered site located at the foot of Mount Sinai. This made our climb more meaningful, creating an unforgettable trip that included physical challenges, natural beauty, and deep reflection.

As we approached the monastery, the sun fully emerged, casting a warm glow over the historic buildings. The serene ambiance of the surroundings invited us to pause and appreciate the spiritual significance of this sacred place.

St. Catherine Cathedral

Saint Catherine's Monastery, located in Egypt's Sinai Peninsula, is the oldest Christian monastery still continuously occupied. It dates back to between 548 and 565 AD. It's located at the base of Mount Sinai.

This place is widely believed to be the exact location where Moses witnessed the awe-inspiring burning bush. The Codex Sinaiticus, an ancient manuscript of the Christian Bible, was preserved here until the mid-19th century. Then, it was moved to the British Library.

The monastery holds a valuable collection of manuscripts and artifacts, making it an important site for religious and historical research. Today, it continues to attract scholars, pilgrims, and tourists keen to explore its profound legacy.

Practical tips

Mt. Sinai Mount Sinai is accessible by road, bus, taxi, and private tours services.

Wear sturdy hiking boots or sneakers to ensure your safety when you hike up the mountain.

If you visit during sunrise or sunset, dress in layers as the temperatures at the summit can be quite cold.

Bring some money, because there are many huts along the path that sell refreshments.

Additionally, consider hiring a local guide who can provide valuable insights into the historical and cultural significance of the area. As you make your way to the summit, take the time to appreciate the breathtaking landscapes that surround you.

Spectacular Sinai

In twilight's hush, where desert whispers call,
Stands Sinai's peak, majestic, vast, and tall.
Upon its heights, where skies and earth entwine,
Lies ancient tales, where sacred paths align.

Beneath the stars, in quiet reverie,
Mount Sinai rises, timeless, wild, and free.
Its rugged slopes, in shadows deeply cast,
Hold secrets of the ages, echoes of the past.

Eagles soar and winds of wisdom speak,
On Sinai's crest, the humble and the meek.
Crimson dawns and dusks of amber gold,
Embrace the mount, where ancient truths unfold.

A beacon bold, in sands of shifting time,
Spectacular Mount Sinai stands, sublime.
A testament of faith, a monument of grace,
In every heart, its sacred, holy place.

www.drandrewcskoh.com/poems

Chapter 7
Dead Sea: Oasis and Mud Therapy

Dead Sea

Years ago, I visited the Dead Sea with a group of adventurous travelers. The Dead Sea is located between Jordan to the east and Israel/Palestine to the west. It is known for its extremely salty water, healing properties, and historical importance. Visiting the Dead Sea was an unforgettable experience, offering relaxation, exploration, and a profound connection to ancient history. The stunning landscape captivated me; the bright blue waters against the dry mountains were breathtaking.

Journey to the Dead Sea

Our tour coach drove through the Judean Desert to set the scene for our unforgettable journey. For our day-trip adventure we checked in at an all-inclusive resort hotel which served as an ideal hub. I was immediately mesmerized by the stunning sights of the Dead Sea. Its sparkling blue waters beautifully contrasted with the desert scenery.

The hotel was luxurious and offered comfortable accommodations and a variety of amenities for an indulgent experience. Once settled, we were excited to explore the Dead Sea's unique buoyancy and healing qualities. Dipping my toes in the mineral-rich waters brought me a calming sense of peace, perfect for the day ahead.

Dead Sea has Unique Characteristics to offer

Located at the Earth's lowest point, the Dead Sea displays outstanding features. It is 306 meters below sea level. Despite its name, the Dead Sea is not actually a sea, but a lake. It serves as the final destination for the Jordan River, with no outlet for the water to flow out.

The Dead Sea is world renowned for its extreme salinity, which is about 10 times that of ocean waters. This high salt concentration creates buoyancy that makes swimming here similar to floating. I entered the Dead Sea with my swimming gear and discovered that I could effortlessly float in the water! It was simply not possible to sink! The experience of it was absolutely surreal and immensely enjoyable!

After emerging from the water, I coated my entire body, from head to toe, with the black mud. This ritual not only makes me unique but also connects me to the earth in a powerful and transformative way!

Lying on the warm shore, I felt rejuvenated as the sun dried my mud-covered skin. The salty water and mineral-rich mud left me feeling relaxed and rejuvenated, as if I were shedding my burdens.

Therapeutic Benefits

The mineral-rich waters and mud of the Dead Sea have long been revered for their therapeutic benefits. The mix of magnesium, sodium, potassium, and bromine is believed to make the skin healthier. It may also reduce arthritis symptoms and promote overall well-being. I absolutely adored indulging in luxurious mud baths and then rinsing off in the salty waters. It truly revitalized and rejuvenated my skin!

The soothing experience not only left my skin feeling silky smooth but also calmed my mind and spirit. Each moment spent in those healing waters felt like a retreat for both body and soul. As I left the baths, the sun's warmth embraced me, enhancing my sense of tranquility. It was a serene escape that lingered long after, reminding me of the importance of self-care and relaxation.

Historical and Cultural Significance

The Dead Sea region is rich with history and religious significance. The Dead Sea area has ancient archaeological sites that show glimpses of past civilizations. The Dead Sea has always fascinated people and attracted pilgrims and travelers looking for its healing powers and historical riches. The area's unique geological formations and natural wonders continue to captivate visitors from around the world.

4,000 years ago, the ancient cities of Sodom and Gomorrah were destroyed by an earthquake near the Dead Sea. Beneath the surface of the Dead Sea are the remains of these cities. The Biblical story of Lot's wife turned into a pillar of salt is powerful and continues to captivate readers.

Exploring the region unveils a rich tapestry of history interwoven with myth and legend. Adventurers along the shores feel the deep connection between the land and the stories that have influenced human history.

Other Activities and Attractions

Beyond floating and mud baths, the Dead Sea area boasts an array of activities and attractions.

Masada

Nearby, is the Masada fortress, a UNESCO World Heritage Site, which tells of Jewish zealots' last stand against Roman rule.

Ein Gedi Nature Reserve

This oasis in the desert features beautiful hiking trails, waterfalls and diverse wildlife.

Qumran Caves

Discovering the Dead Sea Scrolls offers fascinating insight into ancient Jewish history.

Thermal Spas

There are various resorts and spas along the shoreline. They provide exquisite treatments utilizing premium products from the Dead Sea. These products offer an indulgent spa experience.

Practical Tips

For optimal travel conditions, visit between March and May. The weather is milder during this time. You can also visit from September to November. Temperatures tend to be more comfortable then.

Health Precautions

It's important to be careful while shaving before swimming as the salty water may cause a stinging sensation. Also, make sure to avoid getting any water in your eyes.

Hydration and Protection

The extreme heat of the desert can lead to rapid dehydration. Make sure to drink plenty of water. Apply sunscreen to safeguard yourself against the intense sun rays.

Conclusion

A visit to the Dead Sea is more than just a journey. It's an immersive experience into its natural wonder that has mesmerized humans for millennia.

The Dead Sea offers something for all travelers, including relaxation, health benefits, historical exploration, and unique experiences.

Embrace the magic of the Dead Sea and let its healing waters refresh your body and soul!

Dead Sea Float

Buoyant and free, like a leaf adrift,
In a sea of salt, where shadows lift.
Suspended between earth and sky,
I float on dreams, as time slips by.

No effort needed, no struggle found,
Just peace and stillness all around.
The world recedes, its noise and haste,
Replaced by calm, a serene taste.

In these waters, dense and pure,
I find a solace, deep and sure.
A liquid mirror, reflecting me,
As I float upon eternity.

Horizons blur, with each gentle sway,
Lost in the moment, I drift away.
The Dead Sea holds, in its quiet grace,
A sacred space, a timeless place

www.drandrewcskoh.com/poems

DEAD SEA- 400 m below sea level, the lowest point on earth, enjoyed floating on the hypersaline and applying dead sea mud from head to toes!
Do the things that make you happy
Every moment matters

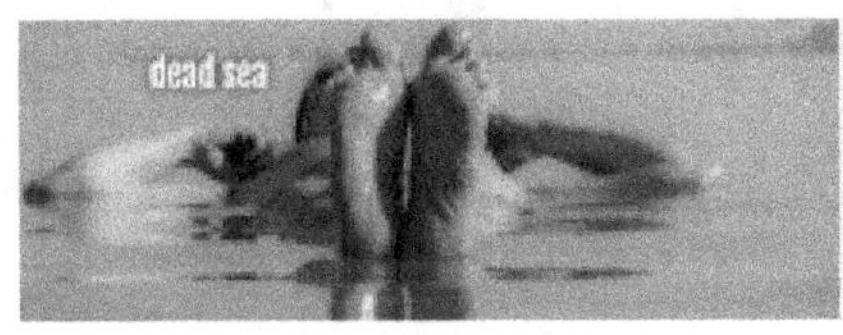

dead sea

Chapter 8
Garden Tomb: Spiritual Pilgrimage

Garden Tomb: "He is Risen, He is not here!"

In 2019, I journeyed to the Garden Tomb in Jerusalem with a group of like-minded pilgrims.

The Garden Tomb is a symbol of spirituality and history outside Jerusalem. In the centre of the complex is an earthen grave carved from rock. Here, pilgrims can engage deeply with the Biblical narrative of Jesus Christ.

As we gathered around the tomb, the atmosphere was charged with reverence and reflection. Each visitor sought their own personal moment of peace, drawing inspiration from the profound significance of this sacred site.

Historical significance

This is a peaceful place to explore spirituality and history through biblical stories and reflection. It is a place to meditate and ponder in beautiful surroundings. It offers a break from the busy city. It facilitates a profound connection with its spiritual essence. It offers a peaceful retreat away from the city's noise, while also offering respite. It welcomes people with its peaceful atmosphere and historical significance for relaxation.

According to Protestant tradition, Jesus Christ could have been buried in this garden. This is a popular tourist destination and pilgrimage site for those seeking peace and spiritual connection. People also flock to the site in search of comfort and to better understand Biblical history. The beautifully maintained gardens provide a serene backdrop for contemplation and prayer. Visitors often leave feeling rejuvenated, carrying with them a sense of peace and a deeper appreciation for their faith.

Back to the past

I entered the gate and saw beautiful gardens. Ancient olive trees encircled a tranquil atmosphere. This place has attracted pilgrims for many years. The meticulously maintained garden features elaborate pathways. These paths lead to the Empty Tomb. It is believed to be where Jesus Christ was buried.

I walked inside this tomb and experienced the solemn atmosphere and of this sacred place firsthand. As I closed my eyes, I was transported back to the past through the time tunnel of my imagination. II envisioned myself in the very spot where the esteemed Apostle John once stood. He saw an extraordinary event two millennia ago. Apostle John saw the empty burial cloths of the Lord and believed that He had risen from the dead.

Exploring the grounds

The Garden Tomb tour begins with a stroll through the lush gardens. This tranquil atmosphere invited me to stop, think about the historical and spiritual significance, and create a unique pilgrimage experience. The paths meander through carefully maintained vegetation, providing a quiet reflection in a busy city environment. As I paused to ponder on the biblical stories, I felt a sense of respect and chose to stay silent.

The Tomb within the Garden Tomb Complex is hewn from the natural rock of a cave. The tomb entrance is well-preserved and leads to a small room with a flat table. The Tomb is made of natural stone and has a simple design. Its surface is akin to Jewish burial caves from the 1st century. The interior is quiet and cool, allowing me to think about the events of two millennia past. The large round stone that can be rolled across the entrance is nearby.

I can imagine the solemnity that surrounded this place, filled with reverence and sorrow. The whispers of history linger here, inviting reflection on those who once found solace in these walls.

Contemplation and Spirituality

The Garden Tomb is a peaceful space to pray, meditate, think, worship, and contemplate in the midst of nature's beauty. Sitting in the tranquil Garden Tomb, I felt a strong connection to its rich history and spirituality. The garden's quietness made me feel calm and filled me with reverence. I could fully concentrate on my thoughts and prayers.

Our group conducted a worship service in the chapel. We took part in Holy Communion and collected an offering to donate to the center. The sense of community and the act of giving back added a deeper layer of significance to my visit. While singing hymns and participating in this sacred tradition, I was reminded of the enduring strength of faith and compassion.

As we shared moments of reflection, the atmosphere was filled with warmth and unity among us. Each voice joined in harmony, creating an uplifting spirit that resonated through the chapel.

Golgotha

Near the Garden tomb is a rock formation on a hill that resembled a man's face. According to Protestant tradition, this is Golgotha, the place of the skull, where Jesus was crucified on Good Friday. This site made my experience more powerful, strengthening my bond with the historical and spiritual importance of the site. Standing before the hill, I couldn't help but feel a profound connection to the events that unfolded there. The weight of history enveloped me, reminding me of the sacrifices made and the hope that followed.

As I stood before it, I couldn't help but feel the weight of centuries of faith and devotion. It was as if the prayers of countless souls echoed in the air, urging me to reflect on my own journey of faith. I realized this place was more than just a destination; it was a sacred symbol of love, suffering, and redemption.

I closed my eyes. I imagined the Lord speaking to one of the thieves on the cross. He said, *"Today, you will be with me in paradise."*

Biblical significance

The Garden Tomb and Golgotha are important places in Christian history and theology.

They represent the key beliefs of resurrection, redemption, and salvation through Jesus Christ's life, death, and resurrection.

Visitors engage deeply with biblical narratives by exploring these significant sites. Visitors can immerse themselves in the profound stories that shaped Christianity as they explore these significant sites.

It provides a tangible and meaningful way to deepen faith and understanding of the central tenets of Christianity.

Practical information

Location

Conrad Schick Street, Jerusalem

Opening Hours

Monday to Saturday, 8:00 AM to 5:30 PM (Closed on Sundays and major Jewish holidays)

Entrance Fee

Minimal fee for guided tours; donations are welcomed.

Conclusion

The Garden Tomb complex is a peaceful place to pray and meditate. This is a sacred site for Christians worldwide. Christians worldwide visit this site to honor important events. These events are at the core of their beliefs. The peaceful and serene atmosphere invites contemplation and a deep sense of spiritual connection.

Golgotha is a place to think and remember Jesus's sacrifice. It marks the end of his earthly life. It also signifies the beginning of a new age in Christian doctrine. This sanctuary evokes deep introspection and spiritual renewal. I can think about Jesus's words to the thief on the cross. It also helps me contemplate my faith journey. I found peace and hope in the promise of paradise, surrounded by greenery and peaceful areas.

I felt incredibly fortunate for having the opportunity to personally witness the profound sacredness of this location. It is here that faith and history gracefully merge, weaving a captivating narrative brimming with inspiration, redemption, and boundless hope.

Garden Tomb

In this hallowed place, where faith and history entwine,
The Garden Tomb stands, a sanctuary divine.
Where once a stone was rolled, revealing hope's embrace,
A promise of resurrection, of everlasting grace.

Golgotha's shadow lingers, just a stone's throw away,
Where love's ultimate sacrifice forever holds sway.
Yet in this sacred garden, where the past meets today,
Hope blooms eternal, in every heartfelt prayer we say.

Pilgrims come from distant lands, seeking to explore,
The Garden Tomb's tranquility, its essence to adore.
With each step they take, on this spiritual quest,
They find renewal, in the peace that here rests.

O Garden Tomb, where heaven's light softly gleams,
A place where faith's journey transcends earthly dreams.

https://www.drandrewcskoh.com/poem

Golgotha

Chapter 9
Petra: A UNESCO Heritage Site

Petra

Discover the breathtaking beauty and historical significance of Petra, Jordan's most famous archaeological site. My trip to Petra, a UNESCO World Heritage Site, showcased its rich culture and history, from the iconic Treasury to ancient tombs.

My visit to Petra, Jordan, was an unforgettable experience. From walking through the famous Siq to standing in awe before the Treasury, Petra's timeless beauty and ancient history left a profound impact on me. Join me as I explore this archaeological wonder, uncovering its secrets and marveling at its grandeur.

Petra, called the *"Rose City"* because of its pink cliffs, is one of the world's most revered archaeological sites. Situated in southern Jordan and dating back to 4th Century BC, Petra became one of the New Seven Wonders of the World during my travels through Jordan recently - it truly felt like traveling through time! As part of my visit, I visited this breathtaking historical marvel that truly took my breath away!

Arrival at Petra

My visit to Petra began early in the morning to avoid the crowds and appreciate its peaceful beauty during quieter times. Upon reaching its entrance, I headed toward Siq - a narrow gorge leading into Petra with towering cliffs and winding pathways that create anticipation for what lies ahead - and started walking through it myself. It's difficult not to picture all the traders and travelers who walked this path thousands of years ago.

As I walked deeper into the Siq, the play of light and shadow on the rock faces created an almost ethereal atmosphere, enhancing the sense of connection to the past. The air was filled with an ancient stillness, reminding me that this was once a thriving hub of commerce and culture, now preserved in time.

As I emerged from the Siq, the breathtaking sight of the Treasury came into view, its intricate façade carved into the rose-red rock. The stunning architecture left me in awe, a testament to the skill and artistry of the Nabataeans.

The Treasury: Petra's Most Iconic Landmark

At the end of Siq, suddenly there it was: Petra's most iconic landmark, Al-Khazneh (The Treasury). Carved into the cliff, its facade features stunning Nabatean architecture, including impressive columns and intricate sculptures, making this monument iconic to Petra.

The golden hues of the setting sun illuminated its features, casting long shadows that danced across the ground. I felt a deep respect, as if I were witnessing history, experiencing the stories held within these ancient walls.

Standing before the Treasury was an eye-opening experience; I was taken aback at its scale and craftsmanship. Originally believed to be a royal tomb, local legends suggest it may also have been used to hide treasure. Whatever its function may have been, however, the Treasury remains an iconic symbol of ancient Nabateans' ingenuity and creativity.

Exploring Petra's Tombs and Monuments

After visiting the Treasury, I continued exploring Petra, wanting to see more of this ancient city. Petra is vast, boasting numerous tombs, temples and monuments dotted throughout its landscape. I enjoyed walking along the Street of Facades, where tombs carved into rock reveal stories of past residents and showcase various designs and scales.

At the Monastery (Al-Deir), I was impressed by its grandeur, rivalling the Treasury in size and beauty. I climbed steep steps to reach the top, and the breathtaking view of the surrounding mountains and valleys was worth it. Like its counterpart Treasury, Al-Deir serves as testimony of Nabateans' skill at carving these monumental structures from rugged terrain.

Petra's Rich History

Petra's history is as compelling as its architecture. Petra, once the capital of the Nabatean Kingdom and a key trade center between East and West, thrived until it came under Roman control in AD 106. The city's significance continued, but its decline began as trade routes shifted, leading to its gradual abandonment. Today, Petra is a UNESCO World Heritage Site and a symbol of resilience and beauty, enchanting all its visitors.

Petra was abandoned by Bedouin tribes in the 7th century after earthquakes damaged its infrastructure. It was rediscovered in 1812 by Swiss explorer Johann Ludwig Burckhardt. Burckhardt's expedition uncovered the lost city for the Western world, igniting interest that led to its preservation. Today, it stands as a testament to the ingenuity of ancient civilizations and the enduring allure of forgotten places.

The Bedouin Connection

While visiting Petra, I met some of the local Bedouin people. Many are descended from ancient Nabateans, making their knowledge of Petra unparalleled. They offered guided tours, shared historical stories, sold handmade crafts and souvenirs, and enriched my experience by teaching me about their lifestyle and heritage preservation efforts.

Their strong connection to the land and its history gave me valuable insights into the significance of Petra. As we walked through the narrow canyon, or Siq, they shared tales that intertwined their ancestry with the very stones surrounding us, breathing life into the ruins.

A Spiritual and Reflective Journey

Petra's historical and architectural importance cannot overshadow its spiritual force. Walking through this ancient city, I felt a strong connection to its past residents and admired their resilience over time, a testament to human strength and perseverance.

Petra is a tranquil spot for reflection, especially at sunset when its vastness is bathed in golden light, creating peaceful moments. More than just a tourist destination, Petra serves as a journey into history's soul.

Each step immersed me in a story filled with ancient history, where every carving and structure revealed secrets of the past. This place inspires a deep respect for the resilience of nature and humanity, highlighting untold stories in overlooked areas.

As I explored Petra, the beautifully crafted facades loomed like silent guardians of a once-thriving civilization. In this captivating atmosphere, I felt a strong urge to discover the mysteries hidden within these ancient walls.

Practical Tips for Visiting Petra

Are You Planning on Travelling to Petra Soon? Here Are a Few Practical Tips That Could Enhance Your Experience:

Visit Petra in the morning to avoid crowds, especially at the Treasury. Wear comfortable shoes for walking in Petra, as the area is large and may require extensive walking.

Stay Hydrated. Petra's desert can be very hot, so bring enough water to keep hydrated while you visit.

As there's so much to see at Petra, take your time exploring. Set aside at least a full day to explore the main landmarks, and consider staying longer for a deeper experience.

Conclusion

My visit to Petra was an unforgettable journey of wonder, history and reflection. The size and beauty of the ancient city deeply impressed me, and its detailed carvings and monuments stayed in my memory. Petra represents more than just history - it stands as testament to human ingenuity and resilience.

No matter your interests - history, adventure or spiritual - Petra offers something special for everyone. I left this ancient city filled with wonder and a deepened appreciation of Nabatean legacy. Petra truly stands as one of the world's great marvels and I highly suggest visiting it when traveling through Jordan.

Jordan
Petra

Chapter 10
Galilee: Museum, Boat Ride, and St. Peter's Fish

Galilee

Visiting the Galilee Boat Museum was a remarkable journey through time. I was captivated by seeing an ancient boat from the era of Jesus. It rested ceremoniously on its original seabed. After this, a serene boat ride across the Sea of Galilee led to a delightful lunch of traditional St. Peter's fish, making the experience unforgettable. This excursion seamlessly intertwined history, spirituality, and the breathtaking beauty of nature.

Visit the Galilee Boat Museum to experience its wonders. Take a scenic boat ride on the serene Sea of Galilee. Indulge in a delightful St. Peter's fish lunch! Immerse yourself in the rich history intertwined with Jesus as you soak in the breathtaking surroundings. Don't miss out, book your adventure today!

Pilgrimage

I traveled to Israel on a pilgrimage. This journey led me to the spiritually and historically rich region of Galilee. This is a place steeped in biblical significance. It's here that Jesus performed many miracles, taught his disciples, and famously walked on water! My visit to the

Galilee Boat Museum was memorable. An unforgettable boat ride across the Sea of Galilee followed it. These experiences created lasting memories. They were beautifully complemented by a delicious lunch of St. Peter's Fish. I am excited to share the highlights of this journey. This will be part of an article. It explores the intertwined themes of history, faith, and local culture!

The Galilee Boat Museum: A Glimpse into the Past

I commenced my journey at Kibbutz Ginosar. It is located on the western shore of the Sea of Galilee. The renowned Galilee Boat Museum, commonly referred to as the "Jesus Boat" Museum, is situated there. This fascinating museum showcases an ancient fishing vessel. It was unearthed during an extended drought between 1986 and 1988. During that time, the water levels of Galilee fell dramatically. The museum showcases an impressive array of exhibits. These exhibits focus on fishing boats uncovered during the recent drought. The highlight is a historic vessel. It is thought to have belonged to fishermen from the time of Jesus.

The Galilee Boat Museum offers a fascinating insight into the region's history. Its exhibits showcase antiquities and artwork. These displays show contemporary life in Galilee. The highlight of the museum is a remarkable boat. It was discovered in 1986 during an unprecedented drought. The water levels had plummeted at that time. This significant find, unearthed amid the exceptionally low waters, serves as a captivating centerpiece of the museum's collection.

The highlight of this remarkable find is a fishing vessel. It dates back to the time period in question. It was unearthed during a severe drought that significantly lowered water levels in the Galilee region. This fascinating discovery occurred in 1986, when the exceptionally low water levels revealed the vessel, later put up for auction.

This vessel is widely known as the "Jesus Boat." It originates from the 1st century AD, a period when Jesus and His disciples walked the earth. There is no direct evidence connecting this particular boat to Jesus Himself. Yet, its discovery provides Christian pilgrims with a remarkable connection to biblical narratives. It evokes imagery of disciples like Peter, Andrew, James, and John embarking on fishing journeys in similar boats. This artifact serves as compelling evidence of the biblical stories, enriching the significance of pilgrimages to these sacred sites.

Seeing the boat up close was truly awe-inspiring. The museum excels in preserving and showcasing this historical artifact, offering insights into its discovery and the conservation techniques used. I was in awe of its incredible condition after centuries submerged beneath the sea, entombed in layers of sediment. The sight of its simple, aged wooden structure was weathered by time. This stirred a deep sense of reverence within me. I contemplated the countless souls who once steered it through its waters.

Boat Ride on the Sea of Galilee: A Spiritual Experience

After my visit to the museum, I began a transforming spiritual journey aboard a boat. We traveled across the tranquil Sea of Galilee, also referred to as the Sea of Tiberias. This captivating expanse of water is famed for being the backdrop of extraordinary miracles performed by Jesus. He calmed tempests and walked on its surface. As our boat gracefully sailed over the shimmering waters, I was filled with a profound sense of peace. I felt awe, realizing I was traversing the same waters once graced by Jesus and his disciples.

The boat ride was a serene escape, providing breathtaking views of the surrounding hills and distant shores. The cool breeze, coupled with the gentle lapping of water against the boat, crafted a peaceful atmosphere perfect for reflection. Gazing over the calm waters brought back cherished childhood stories from biblical texts. This transformed my experience into a deeply personal journey. It became spiritually enriching.

Every wave seemed to carry whispers of ancient tales, reminding me of the faith that has endured through the ages. The sun began to set, casting warm hues across the horizon. I felt a renewed sense of connection to the sacred history that unfolded on these shores.

Our guide invited us to partake in a moment of serene reflection and prayer. After this, we delved into the Gospels. We explored the miraculous deeds of Jesus on the Sea of Galilee. This experience was truly unforgettable. It beautifully bridged the connection between the sacred site and the scriptures. It breathed life into the stories in a way that mere words could never achieve. The anointed guide enchanted everyone with beautiful Christian hymns, harmoniously accompanied by the gentle strumming of a guitar.

St. Peter's Fish Lunch: A Taste of Galilee

After our boat ride, we made our way to a nearby restaurant to savor a Galilean specialty—St. Peter's fish, also known as tilapia. This dish has been cherished by Galileans for centuries. It is named after Peter, one of Jesus' closest disciples. Peter was a fisherman before joining Him as an apostle.

Dining at this restaurant by the shores of the Sea of Galilee was an exquisite experience. Its stunning beauty enhanced it. I chose St. Peter's fish. It was expertly grilled with fresh herbs. A delightful array of Middle Eastern sides like hummus, salads, and pita bread accompanied it. The fish was cooked to perfection. It had a light, flaky texture and a subtle yet distinct freshness. This truly elevated the meal!

As I enjoyed my delightful meal, I contemplated its profound significance in biblical narratives. I remembered the miraculous occasion when Jesus fed thousands with just a few fish and loaves of bread. This dish was simple yet exquisite. It enriched my spiritual journey. It offered me a unique chance to savor a piece of its rich history and cultural heritage.

The Spiritual Significance of Galilee

Galilee resonates deeply with Christians worldwide. It serves as a profound backdrop for many miracles performed by Jesus. It also embodies the essence of His teachings. I have ventured through its serene landscapes. I immersed myself in its spiritual ambiance. Now, I truly understand why Jesus selected this remarkable region to launch His ministry.

The rolling hills and tranquil waters of Galilee show a sense of peace and divine connection that transcends time. Each moment spent there deepened my appreciation for the stories that unfolded in this sacred land. It reminded me of the enduring power of faith and community.

As I walked along the shores of the Sea of Galilee, I could almost hear the echoes of ancient prayers. Praises that filled the air centuries ago were nearly audible. This journey enriched my understanding of the past. It also inspired me to cultivate a deeper sense of gratitude in my own spiritual practice.

My pilgrimage experience was truly extraordinary. It was made memorable by the Galilee Boat Museum. I enjoyed a serene boat ride on the Sea of Galilee and a delightful St. Peter's fish lunch. These moments let me delve into biblical history. I also savored the natural beauty and rich cultural heritage of this stunning region.

Practical Tips for Your Galilee Visit

Plan ahead

The Galilee Boat Museum is immensely popular with Christian pilgrims. Arriving early in the day can help you experience it without the hustle and bustle of large crowds.

Dress comfortably

To fully enjoy both indoor and outdoor activities, choose breathable footwear. Wear light clothing during the warmer months. Especially consider airy fabrics for boat rides.

Bring Your Bible

As you enjoy the boat tour, having a Bible or a scripture app on hand will undoubtedly enhance your journey.

Enjoy Local Cuisine

Don't miss the chance to savor the exquisite St. Peter's Fish.

Conclusion

I visited the Galilee Boat Museum. The serene boat ride across the Sea of Galilee accompanied the visit. These experiences were incredibly enriching. They significantly heightened my appreciation of its biblical significance. Seeing the ancient vessel was unforgettable. It was famously referred to as the "Jesus Boat." It gracefully floated over the still waters. To enhance this remarkable journey, indulging in a delicious lunch of St. Peter's fish deepened my connection to the fascinating tapestry of history, spirituality, and culture that Galilee uniquely presents!

Galilee is an essential destination for any Christian pilgrimage to Israel. Here, the stories of the Bible come to life. Visitors experience a profound sense of peace. The spiritual richness here is unmatched anywhere else. The vibrant landscapes and historical landmarks serve as constant reminders of the region's deep-rooted heritage. The experience gave me a deeper understanding of my faith. It left me with a longing to return to this sacred place.

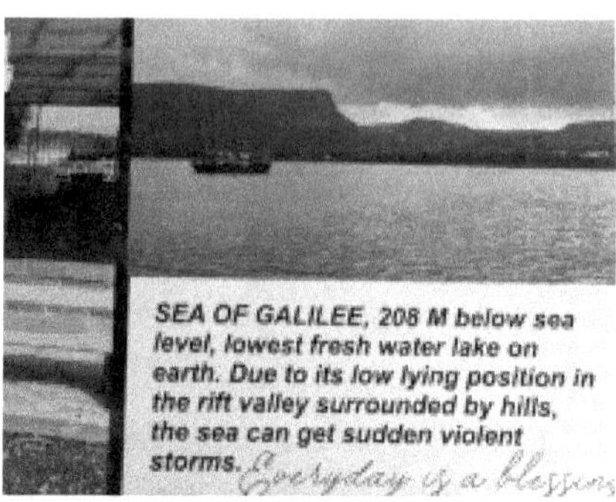

SEA OF GALILEE, 208 M below sea level, lowest fresh water lake on earth. Due to its low lying position in the rift valley surrounded by hills, the sea can get sudden violent storms. Everyday is a blessing

ST PETER'S FISH LUNCH (LEFT)
cheers
MT BENTAL (R)

SEA OF GALILEE

THE
ANCIENT
BOAT
←
Ancient Galilee
Boat
a blessing

Chapter 11
Western Wall: Prayer, and Reflection

Western Wall

Explore my spiritual experience at the Western Wall in Jerusalem, a place known for its historical and cultural importance.

My visit to the Western Wall in Jerusalem was a profoundly inspiring experience, steeped in centuries of faith and devotion. Standing before this ancient stone structure created an incredible, unforgettable spiritual moment that deeply resonated within me.

Sacred Site

My trip to the Holy Land became even more meaningful. I visited the Western Wall, also known as the Wailing Wall, in Jerusalem's Old City. This sacred site is deeply cherished by Jews, Christians, and individuals of various faiths. Standing before the ancient stones, I felt a deep sense of history and a strong connection to the divine. This experience became one of the most unforgettable moments of my journey.

Significance of the Western Wall

The Western Wall is very important in Judaism. It reminds us of the Temple. Roman forces sadly destroyed the Temple in 70 AD. The site is regarded as the holiest in Judaism. It is located nearest to the inner sanctuary (Holy of Holiest) where God's presence once dwelled. For centuries, Jews have gathered here to pray and remember the Temple's destruction, expressing their grief and seeking divine guidance.

The Western Wall holds significant value for Christians and Jews alike, due to Jerusalem's pivotal importance in the Abrahamic faiths. This site is important for pilgrims and attracts tourists seeking spiritual growth or to enjoy its beauty.

The experience of standing before the Wall can evoke profound emotions. Visitors often leave notes and prayers wedged between its ancient stones. This act of connection has created a tradition that transcends generations. It reinforces the Wall's role as a symbol of hope and resilience for countless individuals.

Approaching the Wall: A Moment of Reflection

As I neared the Western Wall, I was overwhelmed by its profound sanctity. Men and women stood before the ancient stones in separate areas. Some bowed their heads with hands clasped in prayer. Others silently wept. Many recited verses from the Torah or Psalms. Over the years, countless visitors had tucked small slips of paper into the crevices of the stones. These papers were filled with heartfelt prayers. Each one is a testament to their deep reverence for this sacred site.

I paused before stepping into the prayer area. I honored Jewish tradition by placing a kippah on my head. This is customary for male visitors. I then approached the wall. Others were there to find peace and seek guidance. We all sought a deep connection with God.

As I stood before the imposing limestone blocks, an overwhelming sense of awe and reverence washed over me. These ancient stones have observed countless moments of triumph, tragedy, and enduring faith over the millennia. I pressed my hand against their cool, sturdy surface. I closed my eyes and silently offered a prayer. I felt a profound sense of spiritual connection and peace envelop me.

I imagined the prayers of countless souls that had come before me as my thoughts drifted. Each prayer was infused with hope and yearning. At that moment, I felt part of something far greater. It was like a tapestry woven through time. This tapestry binds us all in faith and resilience.

The Power of Prayer

One of the most profound experiences at the Western Wall is observing the way visitors unite in prayer. Jewish families celebrate bar and bar mitzvahs. Tourists engage in quiet introspection. Each individual contributes their personal prayers. These are written on scraps of paper and are lovingly tucked into the wall's crevices. This remarkable act stands as a powerful testament to hope and faith. It showcases the shared humanity that binds us all together.

I arrived with a heartfelt prayer written on a small note. I was fully aware that it would become a cherished offering in this sacred space. Here, prayers from around the world converge. Leaving a piece of myself at the Western Wall was profoundly moving. I joined countless others who have done the same.

As I stepped back from the wall, I felt a sense of connection to those who had come before me. I also felt connected to those who would come after. Each person seeks solace and strength in their own unique way. It was a reminder that despite our differences, the essence of prayer transcends boundaries. It speaks to a universal longing for peace and understanding.

Western Wall Plaza

The Western Wall Plaza, the expansive space before the wall, is a captivating nexus where spirituality intertwines with daily life. Men donning tallit (prayer shawls) sway rhythmically in prayer. Groups of women on the opposite side engage in quiet supplications. Some softly sing as they connect with God. This vibrant area gathers families for celebrations like weddings, bar mitzvahs, and various religious ceremonies. These events infuse the atmosphere with a rich tapestry of tradition and emotion.

During my visit, I saw a vibrant bar mitzvah celebration. The young boy stood proudly before the Western Wall, surrounded by his family and friends. The joyful singing and dancing intertwined with the prayer services. This created an atmosphere that was both festive and deeply spiritual. This truly made the place exceptional.

The sun dipped below the horizon. The golden light illuminated the ancient stones. It cast a warm glow over the assembled crowd. The celebration marked the boy's coming of age. It also strengthened the bond of community and faith that the Western Wall symbolizes.

The Historical and Cultural Significance

The Western Wall is more than just a place of prayer. It is a monument with rich historical and cultural importance. Excavations in the surrounding area have unearthed layers that date back to the First and Second Temple periods. These layers reveal ancient streets, tunnels, and artifacts. They offer profound insights into Jerusalem's storied past.

While exploring the area, I deepened my understanding of the wall's importance to Jewish tradition and Israeli society. I also ventured into the Western Wall Tunnels. They run alongside the wall. These tunnels offer fascinating insights into its architectural history and the construction of the Second Temple.

I stood in the tunnels. I could almost hear the echoes of the countless prayers. They have been uttered there throughout the centuries. This experience enriched my appreciation for the site's significance. It also connected me more deeply to the shared heritage of those who hold it dear.

Practical Tips for Visiting the Western Wall

Dress Modestly

Due to its significance as a religious site, it is crucial to dress modestly when visiting the Western Wall. Men should wear a kippah, while women should make sure their shoulders and knees are properly covered.

Respect Prayer Sections

Men and women pray separately at the prayer walls, so please honor this separation when visiting.

Bring Your Prayers

You are welcome to write a personal prayer. Leave it at this sacred site by placing them in the crevices of the wall. Many believe such prayers hold extraordinary significance. For a more tranquil and introspective experience, consider visiting either early in the morning or late in the evening. This approach not only reduces the presence of crowds but also enhances your time for reflection at each location.

Conclusion

My visit to the Western Wall was unforgettable. I explored its profound history. I saw the unwavering faith of countless pilgrims who have stood before it. This sacred site offers a remarkable chance for reflection and prayer. It also provides a deep connection with God and humanity.

Any traveler to Jerusalem must take the opportunity to immerse themselves in this extraordinary site. Here, the ancient seamlessly intertwines with the modern. This creates a profound atmosphere. Spiritual faith and prayer are palpably expressed in every corner.

The Western Wall serves as a testament to resilience and hope, inviting visitors to pause and contemplate their own journeys. It stands as a bridge between the past and present. It reminds us of the enduring power of faith and community.

Visitors approaching the Wall often feel the weight of history enveloping them. Each prayer whispered into its crevices echoes countless others before. This sacred experience fosters personal introspection. It also cultivates a sense of belonging among all who gather, regardless of their backgrounds.

The path to salvation

In a world of darkness, a light breaks through,
A promise of hope, a love so true.
From heaven above, God sent His Son,
To save the lost, the broken one.

Jesus walked the earth with grace untold,

Healing the sick, making the weak bold.
He spoke of a kingdom, not of this place,
Where mercy and love show God's face.

On a cross of shame, He bore our sin,
Dying a death meant for us.
Yet in His sorrow, He gave us grace,
Forgiving all, every fall, every place.

Three days passed, the stone rolled away,

Death defeated, the price now paid.
He rose in glory, He lives again,
Conquering sin, our Savior, our friend.

This is the gospel story of love,
A call to the nations, from heaven above.
Believe in Jesus, accept His grace,
Find life eternal in His embrace.

Spread the word, let every heart hear,
The gospel message, so precious, so clear.

In Christ alone, we find our way,
To live in His light, forever to stay.

www.drandrewcskoh.com/poems

Chapter 12
Qumran Caves: Dead Sea Scrolls

Qumran Caves

Join me as we discover the ancient site where the Dead Sea Scrolls were unearthed: Qumran Caves! Explore the historical importance of this sacred space while unlearning its significance in early Jewish culture and spirituality.

Visiting the Qumran Caves gave me a deep sense of history. This is where the iconic Dead Sea Scrolls were uncovered centuries ago. I explored this archaeological site near the Dead Sea. I felt the deep history of faith and knowledge. The mysteries in the nearby desert caves were palpable.

Dead Sea Scrolls

On my trip to the Holy Land, I visited many interesting and historical places. One of them was the Qumran Caves. These caves are located near the northwestern shores of the Dead Sea. This desert landscape is famous because archaeologists found the Dead Sea Scrolls here. This discovery is one of the greatest archaeological findings ever. Exploring the caves and ancient ruins was captivating. I felt like I had traveled back in time to a secluded Jewish community. This community focused on spiritual purity and left me a valuable legacy. This legacy still resonates today.

The Historical Significance of the Qumran Caves

In 1947, a young Bedouin shepherd discovered ancient scrolls in clay jars at Qumran. This discovery brought global attention to the site. The Dead Sea Scrolls are important Jewish texts from the 3rd century BCE to the 1st century CE. They offer profound insights into early Jewish life, beliefs, and the development of Hebrew scriptures.

The Essenes, a Jewish monastic group, are believed to have copied the scrolls. They lived in Qumran from the 2nd Century BCE to the 1st Century CE. They wanted to escape the political and religious conflicts of Jerusalem and found safety in the Qumran Caves. Their scrolls offer a profound glimpse into their beliefs, rituals, and everyday existence.

The discovery of the Dead Sea Scrolls also reshaped our understanding of the historical context in which early Christianity emerged. Scholars studying these texts uncover a complex religious thought that predates and may influence the New Testament.

My Journey to Qumran Caves

As I neared Qumran National Park, I was captivated by the striking beauty of the Judean Desert. The arid terrain was punctuated by caves etched into the rocky cliffs, each one safeguarding secrets from a long-lost era. The barren landscape felt tranquil, revealing stories of the people who once lived and worshiped here.

My visit commenced with an exploration of the remarkable ruins of the Qumran Settlement. I toured its expansive communal dining room, explored the ritual baths (mikvahs), and walked through the living quarters. I immersed myself in the remnants of this fascinating site. These structures clearly show the Essene lifestyle, marked by strict religious practices like daily ritual baths and purposeful communal meals.

I continued my journey. The surrounding silence intensified. It made me envision the vibrant daily life that once filled these walls. In the shadow of the cliffs, I could almost hear the faint echoes of ancient prayers and discussions.

The Caves: A Gateway to the Past

I explored the main settlement of Qumran. Then, I went to the famous caves that hid the Dead Sea Scrolls for centuries. These caves, nestled among the cliffs encircling Qumran, are many; yet, not all are accessible to visitors. Standing outside a closed entrance made me imagine the Essenes protecting their sacred scrolls from destruction.

The view inside the caves was stunning. The sparkling waters of the Dead Sea beautifully contrasted against the towering desert cliffs. The Essenes chose this remote location for their community to avoid urban distractions. This seclusion allowed them to focus entirely on their spiritual practices.

I looked deeper into the cave's shadows. I could almost feel the echoes of ancient prayers. Rituals once filled the space. Every crevice held secrets of a past era. They invited me to discover the stories of those who once lived. Those people found comfort in these rugged walls.

The Discovery of the Dead Sea Scrolls

The finding of the Dead Sea Scrolls in 1947 captured global interest and was an important event in biblical archaeology. These ancient texts contain fragments from almost every book of the Hebrew Bible. They also include writings that reveal the beliefs and practices of the Essenes.

I explored the caves and thought about an incredible discovery. Over seventy years ago, a shepherd found these important manuscripts. Witnessing such a pivotal moment in religious history was truly unforgettable. It left me in awe that these texts have endured for millennia!

The meticulous preservation of the scrolls offers invaluable insights into the cultural and historical context of the time. Each fragment serves as a testament to the resilience of faith and knowledge throughout the ages.

Spiritual Reflection

Visiting the Qumran Caves was not just a learning experience for me. It was a deeply spiritual experience that allowed for significant reflection. The Essenes' strong faith, careful copying of sacred texts, and resilience in tough times greatly impressed me.

The Qumran Caves stand as a powerful testament to faith and humanity's enduring quest for meaning beyond the material realm. Though the Essenes have long vanished, their remarkable legacy endures, inspiring individuals of all faiths. Ancient scrolls found in caves link the past with the present. These scrolls show the significance of scripture. Prayer and devotion are highlighted as important in our lives.

Standing in the rugged terrain, I felt a deep connection to those who sought solitude and enlightenment here. This experience reminded me that the search for understanding and spiritual truth is still relevant today.

Practical Tips for Visiting the Qumran Caves

Time of Visit

Visit between October and April, or go early in the morning to avoid the heat.

What to Bring:

Visitors should bring comfy shoes, sunscreen, a hat, and enough water, as it can get very hot and dry.

How to Reach

You can drive to Qumran National Park in 30-45 minutes from Jerusalem or Tel Aviv. Alternatively, you can choose a guided Dead Sea tour that includes Qumran.

Museum Visit

Visit the museum on-site. You can learn about the Essenes there. You will see the Dead Sea Scrolls and find amazing archaeological artifacts from the area. This engaging experience offers a profound understanding of the lifestyles and beliefs of the communities that once thrived here.

Conclusion

It was an interesting trip to visit the Qumran Caves. It helped me understand the faith and dedication of the Essenes who lived there. Walking in their footsteps allowed me to appreciate their important contributions to ancient Jewish history and biblical texts.

Qumran is a must-visit destination for anyone fascinated by biblical history, archaeology, or spiritual reflection. The caves offer a unique chance to explore an environment that has greatly shaped our understanding of scripture and faith.

This journey has significantly enriched my understanding of history while providing a peaceful environment for personal reflection. It reminds me of the lasting impact these communities have had on our world today.

I wandered through the site. I felt a deep connection to those who once sought solace and enlightenment in these very caves. Each artifact and inscription whispered stories of devotion and perseverance, long echoing through the corridors of time.

The First Will Be Last

In the race of life, we strive and run,
Chasing the light of the rising sun.
We seek to climb, to reach the peak,
Where power and pride are all we
seek.

But the higher we rise, the more we
lose,
The simple truths we once did
choose.
For those who lead, with grasping
hands,
May find their feet on shifting sands.

For in the kingdom, all is reversed,
The last is blessed, the humble first.
The meek will stand where pride
once fell,
And grace will ring the victory bell.

The hands that served, the hearts
that gave,
Will find their place beyond the
grave.
For crowns of gold will fade away,
But love' s pure light will ever stay.

www.drandrewcskoh.com/poems

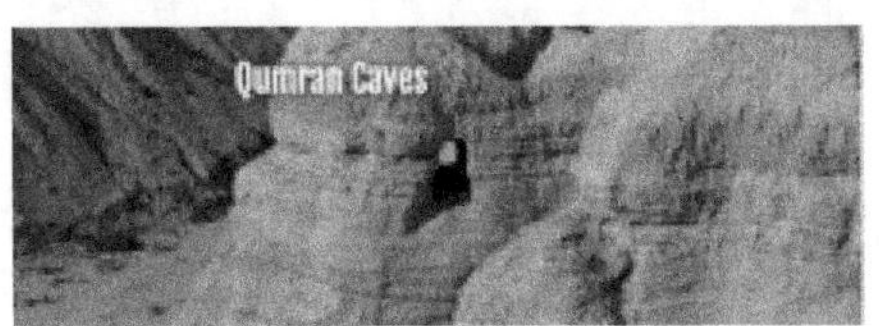
Qumran Caves

Chapter 13
Capernaum: Hometown of Jesus

Capernaum

Discover the ancient town of Capernaum, a pivotal location in Jesus' ministry. Come with me as we delve into its ruins, stand where He taught, and contemplate its profound spiritual importance.

Experiencing Capernaum, the site where Jesus performed many miracles and shared teachings in the synagogue, was profoundly spiritual for me. I walked among its ancient ruins along the shores of the Sea of Galilee. I felt a deep connection to the life and ministry of Jesus.

Hometown of Jesus

During my pilgrimage to the Holy Land, countless moments etched themselves into my memory. Yet, none compared to the awe-inspiring visit to the historical site of Capernaum. Referred to as "Jesus' own city" in the scriptures (Matthew 9:1), this destination held an unparalleled significance. It was within these very walls that Jesus performed breathtaking miracles and imparted his divine teachings within the synagogue. This once humble fishing village is situated gracefully on the serene shores of the Sea of Galilee. It now stands as a testament to the passage of time. It draws devout Christians from every corner of the globe.

As I wandered through the captivating remnants of this ancient marvel, a profound sensation enveloped me. It was as if I had been transported back in time. I felt suspended in an ethereal realm. This allowed me to tangibly connect with the sacred ministry of Jesus that unfolded more than two millennia ago. The profound impact of this experience moved me at my core, leaving an indelible mark on my soul.

Biblical Significance

Capernaum is a pivotal location in the Gospels. It was here that Jesus drew many of His first disciples, including Peter, Andrew, James, and John (Mark 1:16-20). In this vibrant town, He performed a multitude of miracles. He healed a centurion's servant (Luke 7:1-10). He also cast out demons (Mark 1:21-28) and restored health to Peter's mother-in-law (Matthew 8:14-15). Additionally, Capernaum functioned as Jesus' primary base of operations during His ministry in Galilee.

The ancient synagogue is one of the most extraordinary landmarks in Capernaum. This is the place where Jesus delivered His profound teachings. This holy site served as the center of Jewish religious life in Capernaum. As I stood among its ruins, I could vividly imagine the crowds of devoted followers, spellbound by Jesus' compelling sermons.

His voice echoed around me. The sound seemed to linger in the air. It reminded me of the profound impact He had on the lives of those who gathered there. It was a powerful reflection of faith and devotion that continues to inspire many today.

The intricate stonework heightened my sense of reverence in that space. The remnants of the once-grand structure contributed to the atmosphere. Walking through the remains, I couldn't help but contemplate the enduring legacy of spirituality. This legacy continues to resonate in the hearts of believers around the world.

Arriving at Capernaum

As I arrived in Capernaum, the serene shores of the Sea of Galilee greeted me. It was a beautiful setting for deep spiritual reflection. Upon entering the ancient ruins, I was instantly captivated by their remarkable preservation. The moment I stepped into this sacred space, I was overwhelmed by its rich historical and spiritual significance.

As I approached Capernaum, its grand sign proudly proclaiming *"The Town of Jesus"* greeted me. I realized I was stepping into an ancient site steeped in rich history. This place carries deep spiritual significance for Christians around the globe.

The air felt charged with the echoes of past miracles and teachings, inviting me to explore further. Each stone seemed to whisper stories of faith and resilience, urging me to immerse myself in this sacred journey.

I wandered through the remains of ancient homes, imagining the lives once lived within their walls. Each corner held a mystery, beckoning me to uncover the timeless legacy that Capernaum so generously offered.

Exploring the Ancient Synagogue

The highlight of my visit was, without a doubt, discovering an ancient synagogue. It dates back to the 4th or 5th century AD. It stands atop another structure thought to be a place where Jesus Himself taught. The synagogue's stunning white limestone columns and walls contrasted beautifully with the darker basalt stones in the surrounding area. This created a striking visual that captivated me. It left me eager to learn more!

As I wandered through the remnants of a synagogue, I paused. I considered its rich history as a site of teaching and healing. I envisioned Jesus standing in the very spot I occupied, sharing the Good News with His followers. It was a profoundly humbling experience to be in a place where His words and actions transformed so many lives.

The echoes of those teachings lingered in the air. They inspired a sense of reverence and connection to the past. I continued to explore the intricate mosaics and ancient inscriptions. I couldn't help but feel grateful for the opportunity to witness such a significant piece of history.

Peter's House: A Key Archaeological Site

Next to the synagogue lies a significant archaeological site believed to be the former home of Peter. Jesus healed Peter's mother-in-law in this very place. This event transformed it into a vital gathering spot for early Christians. Today, a contemporary church has been constructed above the site. It features glass floors. These floors allow visitors to glimpse the ancient remnants lying below.

As I approached Peter's house, I reflected on the deeply personal nature of Jesus' ministry. He didn't just preach to the masses. He engaged with individuals directly. Jesus visited their homes to heal the sick and restore hope. Standing there alongside Peter, I could truly sense the profound connection between Jesus and His followers.

The air felt thick with history, as if the very stones around me held the echoes of those sacred moments. In that poignant silence, I realized how this place symbolized faith. It also represented the enduring power of community. Moreover, it showed the love shared among believers.

The Shores of the Sea of Galilee

After exploring the ancient ruins, I strolled along the serene shores of the Sea of Galilee. Its tranquil waters and the surrounding hills crafted a perfect atmosphere for quiet contemplation. I imagined Jesus calling His disciples to cast their nets into these waters. He then sent them out as *fishers of men* (Mark 1:17).

The Sea of Galilee played a pivotal role in Jesus' ministry. Experiencing the area firsthand deepened my appreciation for its stunning landscape. Its serene atmosphere inspired many Gospel stories. Its beauty and peacefulness created the perfect environment for reflection. The area also provided an ideal setting for teaching.

As I walked along the pebbled shore, the gentle lapping of the waves mirrored the calming sensation within my soul. Each step felt like a journey through time, connecting me to the profound spiritual heritage that this sacred place embodies.

Spiritual Reflection

My visit to Capernaum went beyond a mere educational journey through history. It transformed into a deeply immersive spiritual experience. This experience vividly revived the life and ministry of Jesus. I explored Peter's house, the ruins of the synagogue, and surrounding village structures like Peter's tomb. These explorations breathed new life into the biblical stories I had always known. They reignited my faith in a profound way.

Capernaum resonates deeply with me. It evokes the essence of Jesus' personal approach to ministry. He connected with individuals right where they were, whether in synagogues, homes, or by the sea. It was here that He performed many breathtaking miracles, and shared His transforming message of love and redemption.

I stood by the shores of the Sea of Galilee. I could almost hear His voice echoing in the gentle lapping of the waves. His call to discipleship reminded me deeply. This serene landscape is deeply intertwined with sacred narratives. It served as a backdrop for historical events. It is also a powerful reminder of my own spiritual journey.

Practical Tips

Best Time to visit

The best time to visit Capernaum is from October to April, when temperatures are more moderate. For a more comfortable experience, explore early in the morning during these months. Summer temperatures can soar.

What to Bring

To fully enjoy your exploration of Capernaum, it's crucial to wear comfortable walking shoes. Also, bring along water, a hat, and sunscreen. There are no shaded areas available in this stunning locale.

How to get there

Capernaum is situated along the northern shore of the Sea of Galilee. It can be reached in under two hours by car from Jerusalem. Alternatively, it is within an hour from Nazareth through organized tours.

Admission

The proceeds from admission fees to the archaeological park contribute to its preservation for future generations.

Conclusion

My visit to Capernaum was a captivating experience that deepened my understanding of Jesus's life and ministry. Standing in the synagogue where He taught created a strong connection. Walking along the shores of Galilee strengthened this bond. Exploring the ancient ruins made Scripture and the tangible reality of His existence even more meaningful.

Capernaum is a must-visit destination for any Christian pilgrimage or biblical history tour. It offers a unique glimpse into the life of Jesus and the early Christian communities. It provides ample opportunities for reflection. You will find inspiration and spiritual renewal.

The tranquil ambiance of the surroundings enriches this experience. It enables visitors to completely immerse themselves in the site's historical and spiritual significance. Ultimately, Capernaum stands as a powerful testament to the lasting influence of faith throughout history.

Capernaum

A MONUMENT OF
ST FRANCIS OF
ASISSI IN
CAPERNAUM

A MONUMENT
OF ST PETER
CAPERNAUM

Chapter 14
Magdala: Legacy of Mary Magdalene

Magdala

Explore Magdala, the birthplace of Mary Magdalene, and immerse yourself in its rich biblical heritage. Discover the site's amazing archaeological treasures. These include the beautiful Magdala stone. You can also see the ancient synagogue with views of the Sea of Galilee.

Hometown of Maty Magdala

My visit to Magdala was a captivating journey through history. While at the Sea of Galilee, I explored ancient ruins. These included the Magdala Stone and the Synagogue. I reflected on the site's biblical significance as Mary Magdalene's hometown.

Situated beside the serene waters of Galilee, Magdala is an ancient town rich in biblical significance. This historical site is known as the birthplace of Mary Magdalene, one of Jesus' followers. It invites visitors to explore its sacred ruins. Guests can contemplate on early Christianity's origins there.

Wandering through the town's ruins, I felt the echoes of stories from those who walked these paths long ago. These stories reflected their struggles and triumphs. Each artifact and structure seemed to breathe life into the narratives of faith that have shaped the region for generations.

Arriving at Magdala

Upon my arrival in Magdala, I was instantly enchanted by its tranquil ambiance. Located by the Sea of Galilee, this charming town holds great spiritual and archaeological importance for visitors. A friendly information center welcomes guests, providing insights into Magdala's rich heritage through engaging multimedia presentations and interactive exhibits.

While exploring, I discovered an ancient synagogue, its stones echoing stories of past worship and community gatherings. The intricate floor mosaics were mesmerizing, showcasing the artistry and dedication of those who created them.

Magdala Stone and Synagogue

One of the highlights of my trip was seeing the Magdala stone. It is a remarkable archaeological find believed to be dated before the Second Temple period. The stone features detailed carvings that illustrate Jewish religious practices from Jesus' time.

Beside the stone lies a remarkable first-century synagogue discovered in Israel. Strolling through its crumbling pathways is akin to stepping back in time. The thought that Jesus preached here in the 1st century AD added to its sacred significance.

The atmosphere is filled with reverence, evoking echoes of ancient voices and teachings. Every part of this sacred site shares a story, inviting visitors to connect with its rich history.

Encountering Mary Magdalene's Legacy

Magdala holds profound significance for many Christian pilgrims, particularly because of its connection to Mary Magdalene's legacy. During my visit, I found myself deeply reflecting on this heritage. The "Duc In Altum" spiritual center invites guests to engage in prayer and contemplation. The beautifully designed chapel honored her remarkable legacy.

When I stepped into the chapel, I felt peace. The soft light on the artwork created a sense of connection to the past. Every moment here brought me closer to understanding Mary Magdalene's influence on faith and devotion.

As I explored the serene surroundings, I felt a renewed sense of purpose stirring within me. This journey deepened my appreciation for her story. It inspired me to embrace her spirit of devotion in my own life.

Exploring Archaeological Discoveries

The findings at Magdala reveal much more than just the synagogue. They include parts of a busy marketplace, homes, and other buildings that show daily life in the first century AD. Ongoing excavations offer the thrilling opportunity to witness history being uncovered right before your eyes!

Each artifact tells a story, connecting us to the past in ways we never thought possible. It reminds me of my connection to those who came before me. It encourages me to honor their legacy.

Walking through the site, I can almost hear echoes of past conversations and the bustling marketplace. This connection deepens my appreciation for their remarkable resilience and creativity in shaping the world today.

The Beauty of the Sea of Galilee

No visit to Magdala would be whole without immersing yourself in the serene beauty of the Sea of Galilee. The gentle waves caressing the shore, mixed with the tranquil landscape, create a perfect setting for meditation and spiritual rejuvenation. It's easy to envision Jesus and his disciples strolling along these very shores two thousand years ago!

The stories of their journeys resonate with the warm breeze that carries whispers of history. As the sun sets, it casts a golden hue over the water. One can't help but feel a profound sense of peace and reflection.

I found myself lost in thought, allowing the ambiance to inspire my own personal connections to the past. The Sea of Galilee is visually stunning. It is spiritually uplifting. It highlights the enduring nature of faith and the beauty of the natural world.

Conclusion

My visit to Magdala was an unforgettable journey through biblical history. The ancient synagogue and Mary Magdalene's legacy provided moments for reflection and a genuine link to early Christianity. If you're planning a Christian pilgrimage to Israel, be sure to include Magdala. It brings history to life in meaningful ways.

Magdala offers visitors a chance to connect with Scripture and experience its lasting legacy of faith and tradition. The serene beauty of the surroundings enhances the profound spiritual experience, inviting contemplation and prayer. Overall, Magdala stands as a testament to the enduring impact of faith on culture and heritage.

Exploring its ancient streets, one can feel the echoes of those who walked there centuries ago. This sacred site enhances understanding of biblical history and fosters a personal connection to the stories that shaped Christianity.

The Lord is My Shepherd

The Lord is my Shepherd, I shall not fear,He guides my steps, His voice I hear.In pastures green, He leads me still,Beside the waters, calm and chill.
He restores my soul when I'm worn thin,His love surrounds, His peace within.
Though shadows dark may block my way,With Him, I know I will not stray.
His rod and staff, they comfort me,In His embrace, I am set free.My cup overflows with blessings untold,His mercy follows, His grace I hold.
Through every valley, high and low,He walks beside me, this I know.In Him, my trust, my hope, my song,The Shepherd's love will lead me strong.

www.drandrewcxskoh.com/poems

Chapter 15

En Gedi: Waterfalls and History in the Judean Desert

Engedi

Experience the majestic beauty of En Gedi, an oasis in Israel's Judean Desert. Come discover its long history, cascading waterfalls, wildlife and learn its significance from Scripture during your stay in Israel.

A fascinating journey through a special place in the Judean Desert reveals beautiful waterfalls and old caves. It blends natural splendor with profound spiritual reflection. This experience highlights its historical importance in Israel.

Beautiful Oasis

En Gedi is a beautiful oasis in Israel's Judean Desert near the Dead Sea. It invites visitors to experience a serene escape from the arid landscape. While visiting, they can explore one of the country's most historic and cherished destinations.

Engedi is known for its biblical importance and stunning scenery. It offers a refreshing escape near Jerusalem. Visitors can enjoy nature and explore this cherished location.

Arriving at En Gedi

The striking contrast between the arid landscape of the Judean Desert and the vibrant oasis of En Gedi captivated me. I crossed the dry, rocky landscape and arrived at En Gedi. Then, I experienced lush greenery, winding streams, and the calming sounds of waterfalls.

As I ventured further into the oasis, the air changed. It carried the scent of blooming flowers and the gentle rustle of leaves. Every step uncovered more of En Gedi's treasures, from ancient ruins to vibrant wildlife in this unique sanctuary.

The ancient ruins whispered stories of the past, inviting me to imagine the lives once lived in this enchanting place. I took a moment to enjoy the sunlight streaming through the palm trees. I felt a strong connection to the beauty and history around me.

The Biblical Significance of En Gedi

En Gedi occupies a significant position in biblical history, especially in the narrative of David. In 1 Samuel 24, David sought refuge in En Gedi to escape from King Saul. Although he had the chance to kill Saul, he chose to show mercy and humility instead. As I wandered through its reserve, I vividly imagined the biblical events that unfolded in this remarkable place!

Each step brought me closer to the heart of the stories etched in the stones and hills. The beautiful landscape was mesmerizing. Its rich history made me feel like I was walking alongside the figures who once traveled these paths.

The Song of Solomon highlights this location as a symbol of beauty and abundance, underscoring its profound spiritual importance. As I continued, the scent of blooming flowers reminded me of poems and songs that praised nature's gifts. This connection between nature and faith deepened my appreciation for the sacred narratives tied to this land.

The En Gedi Nature Reserve

The En Gedi Nature Reserve captivates with its stunning landscapes and diverse wildlife. I began my hike on a marked trail.

I enjoyed the beauty of En Gedi. I discovered beautiful waterfalls, refreshing pools, and a variety of local plants.

David's Waterfall, a celebrated natural wonder, provides a serene haven for rest and introspection. I dipped my feet in the refreshing water, enjoying the peace and admiring the lively ecosystem in the desert.

I sat by the waterfall. I felt a deep connection to the surrounding history. I imagined ancient figures who once walked these paths. The peace of En Gedi inspired me to think about the beauty of nature and my spiritual journey.

En Gedi's Wildlife and Natural Beauty

En Gedi is celebrated for its rich biblical history and stunning biodiversity. While hiking in the reserve, I saw ibexes climbing cliffs and rock hyraxes lounging on boulders, completely unbothered by visitors. This vibrant wildlife enhances the area's serene natural beauty, creating a truly harmonious environment.

En Gedi boasts a remarkable collection of rare plants that thrive in its unique desert climate. This oasis offers a captivating blend of Mediterranean and desert vegetation, making it truly remarkable.

The lush greenery stands in stark contrast to the surrounding arid landscape, inviting exploration and discovery. As I wandered through the diverse ecosystem, the tranquil sounds of nature provided a soothing soundtrack to my adventure.

Caves and Archaeological Sites

One of the standout moments of my trip was exploring the caves. It is believed that David sought refuge from Saul in these caves. The ancient caverns in En Gedi offer a captivating look at biblical history. They connect us to events from thousands of years ago. It was truly an extraordinary experience!

En Gedi is famous for its beautiful caves. It also boasts archaeological treasures. These include an ancient synagogue and a village from the Roman and Byzantine periods. These remnants give valuable insights into the historical significance of En Gedi, underscoring its importance in the annals of history.

As I walked through these sites, it felt like the stones were echoing. They seemed to tell the stories of those who once lived here. Each corner revealed new wonders, making it clear why En Gedi remains a focal point for historians and adventurers alike.

Conclusion: A Journey of Beauty and Spirituality

My visit to En Gedi was an incredible experience. It merged history and natural beauty. This created a powerful connection with both. En Gedi offers a unique experience for every visitor. Whether you are a spiritual seeker or an adventure lover, its breathtaking landscapes and diverse wildlife will amaze you.

En Gedi is more than just a desert oasis. It's a haven for refuge, reflection, and renewal in a beautiful natural setting. The ancient tales that weave through this land come alive in remarkable ways. Walking through the lush greenery and waterfalls, I felt a deep sense of peace, highlighting the sacredness of the place. This journey reinforced my belief that nature's beauty can inspire profound spiritual growth and connection.

A trip to En Gedi is essential for anyone visiting Israel. The experience immerses visitors in a serene environment where every corner whispers stories of the past. As I walked along the trails, the stunning views prompted a sense of gratitude for the incredible world we inhabit.

A thousand may fall, Psalm 91
(sing to the tune of 500 miles)

Verse 1
When I wake up, I know He's
there,
In the shelter of the Most High's
care,
In the shadow of Almighty's wings,
I find refuge.

verse 2
A thousand may fall, it won't come
near,
In the darkness, I have no fear.
For His angels guard me dear,
In His love

verse 3
He is my fortress, He is my shield,
In His presence, all my fears are
healed.
when I call on Him, He is near,
no need to fear.

Verse 4
In the shelter of the Most High's
care,
I find refuge, I find peace there.
He is my fortress, He is my shield,
all my fears are healed.

www.drandrewcskoh.com/songs

ENGEDI- literally
"spring of the young
goat"- as the deer
pants for the water,
Psalm 42, also 1 Sam
24

Chapter 16
Shiloh: Israel's Ancient Tabernacle Site

Shiloh

Explore the historical and biblical significance of Shiloh, once the location of Israel's Tabernacle. My visit provides an insightful journey through Israel's rich history, uncovering its profound religious heritage.

My journey to Shiloh, the ancient city that once housed the Tabernacle, was akin to stepping back in time. With its rich archaeological discoveries and profound biblical significance, Shiloh offers a breathtaking glimpse into Israel's spiritual heritage. It is truly an essential destination for both pilgrims and history enthusiasts.

Spiritual Heart of Israel

Shiloh is a site rich in historical and biblical significance, once considered the spiritual heart of Israel. Shiloh is located in the beautiful Samaria hills. It was home to the Tabernacle for over three centuries. The Ark of the Covenant was kept there. During my visit, I was deeply affected by the atmosphere, sensing the ancient spiritual life that once thrived in Israel.

Arriving at Shiloh

The journey to Shiloh begins in Samaria, the biblical region renowned as the hill country of Ephraim. As I arrived at the site, I was impressed by its rich history. The Old Testament often mentions it as a key location for Israel's worship. It was also important for the division of Canaan's land among the tribes.

The ancient ruins of Shiloh tell the stories of its past as a vibrant religious center. Walking among the remnants, I could almost hear the echoes of prayers and rituals that once filled the air.

Each stone seemed to whisper secrets of devotion and faith that resonated through the ages. Immersed in this history, I felt a profound connection to the spiritual journey of those who walked here before me.

Biblical Significance

Shiloh occupies a vital position in the Bible, particularly in the book of Joshua. It was at Shiloh that Joshua set up his Tabernacle upon entering the Promised Land (Joshua 18:1). For centuries, Shiloh functioned as Israel's spiritual capital, hosting significant religious festivals, including the annual pilgrimage celebrations.

Shiloh is renowned as the birthplace of Samuel, the final judge of Israel. It was here that Hannah dedicated her son to God, and Samuel grew up serving under Eli the priest. God's revelation to Samuel occurred in this sacred place. This event marked the beginning of his journey to becoming one of Israel's greatest prophets (1 Samuel 3).

Wandering through Shiloh, I could imagine countless prayers and divine encounters, making my visit extraordinary. The ancient ruins whispered stories of faith and devotion, inviting reflection on the profound legacy of this historic site. I stood among the remains of the past. A deep sense of connection to the generations that had walked this land enveloped me.

Archaeological Discoveries

One of the most fascinating features of Shiloh is the wealth of evidence it has revealed throughout the years. Excavations have uncovered ancient structures, pottery, and artifacts that date back to the era of the Tabernacle in Jerusalem. During my visit, I saw walls, wine presses, and storage areas. These features highlight the site's rich history. They remind us of the vibrant community that once thrived there.

A standout moment of our visit was standing at what is believed to be the site of the Tabernacle itself. Although archaeologists have identified a location that likely once held its platform, no physical remains are visible today. Nonetheless, being there was deeply inspiring and powerful.

The palpable sense of history in the air echoed the stories of those who worshiped and gathered there centuries ago. Every step I took deepened my appreciation for the faith and traditions that have influenced many lives.

Spiritual Reflections

Strolling through the ancient Israelite site of Shiloh enveloped me in peace. The picturesque landscape, adorned with olive trees and gentle rolling hills, exudes a timeless charm that captivates the soul. The ancient Israelites chose Shiloh for their Tabernacle because its peaceful setting is perfect for reflection. It is also ideal for connecting with history and the divine.

Standing at the site of the former Tabernacle, I reflected on its pivotal role in the lives of the Israelites. This sacred place was where they gathered to offer sacrifices, seek divine forgiveness, and God's guidance for their lives. Shiloh served as a profound reminder of God's holiness and the covenant bond He maintained with His people.

As I enjoyed the peaceful surroundings, I could almost hear the prayers and hymns of those who came before me. Each stone and artifact told a story, creating a deep tapestry of faith that touched my heart.

Shiloh Visitor Center

Enhance your visit to Shiloh by stopping at the visitor center. It has an engaging multimedia presentation about the site's history. Discover biblical events related to Shiloh along with recent archaeological findings to enhance your understanding before visiting its impressive ruins.

The center showcases the rich history of worship at this location, displaying artifacts found during excavations. These items create a profound connection to our ancient heritage. Interacting with these artifacts is inspiring. It is also educational. These interactions give visitors a vivid reminder of the site's rich and diverse history. Here, visitors can also experience a hologram of the Ancient Tabernacle.

The visitor center provides guided tours that explore the stories of those who worshiped there, along with the artifacts. This immersive experience allows guests to truly appreciate the significance of Shiloh in both historical and spiritual contexts.

Modern Pilgrimage

Today's pilgrims can follow the journeys of famous biblical figures at Shiloh. Notable figures include Joshua, Samuel, and Eli. Their timeless tales of faith and obedience take on new life. Shiloh is a key destination in Israel for both historical exploration and personal reflection due to its deep spiritual importance.

Shiloh offers visitors a positive spiritual experience and a space for personal reflection on their spiritual journeys. After leaving Shiloh, I was amazed by God's guidance throughout history. He has provided His people with guiding lights of faith.

Walking through this ancient site, I felt a strong connection to the past, highlighting the links in the biblical narrative. Reflecting on these experiences instilled a renewed sense of purpose and commitment to my own spiritual path.

Conclusion: Journey through Time and Faith

My visit to Shiloh was an unforgettable journey that intertwined history and faith. With its profound biblical legacy and archaeological importance, Shiloh holds a pivotal place in Israel. The deep spiritual traditions here testify to this heritage, where ancient spirituality converges with modern beliefs at every corner.

If you're planning a trip to Israel, make sure to add Shiloh to your itinerary. Shiloh offers a meaningful experience for history lovers. It also provides spiritual seekers with lasting impact on your mind and heart.

Walking through the remnants of the past, each step tells a story of devotion and resilience. The sacred atmosphere encourages reflection, prompting you to consider your journey and beliefs in this timeless setting.

Chapter 17
Mount of Beatitudes: Spiritual Retreat

Mount of Beatitudes

Discover the peaceful essence and significance of the Mount of Beatitudes, where Jesus gave his Sermon on the Mount. Delve into its rich history, breathtaking vistas, and deep ties to the Christian faith.

Visiting the Mount of Beatitudes, the site where Jesus delivered His Sermon on the Mount, was an incredibly amazing experience. This beautiful place by the Sea of Galilee offers a peaceful setting. It lets you contemplate on Christ's teachings. You can connect with the spiritual history of the Holy Land.

A Place of Peace and Reflection

The Mount of Beatitudes is rich in spiritual significance. This hilltop near the Sea of Galilee is traditionally known as the location of the Sermon on the Mount. It is said that this is where Jesus gave the Sermon on the Mount. It is also recognized for including the Beatitudes. As I stood atop its slope, a profound sense of peace and reverence enveloped me, emanating from this sacred location.

The beautiful views of the green landscapes by the sea created a peaceful atmosphere, encouraging reflection and gratitude. The wind carried timeless messages of love and compassion from Jesus to His followers.

Arriving at the Mount of Beatitudes

My journey to the Mount of Beatitudes began with a stunning drive through the picturesque Galilee region. Upon arrival, I was captivated by the natural beauty around me, gentle hills and vibrant flowers. The clear waters of the Sea of Galilee created a serene atmosphere. It's no wonder that Jesus selected this breathtaking location for one of His most revered sermons.

The site is well-maintained, with neat pathways leading to beautiful viewpoints and a church honoring Jesus's Sermon on the Mount. The calm atmosphere provides a great escape from everyday stress. It encourages guests to meditate on the lasting importance of the Beatitudes and their messages.

I felt a deep sense of peace that encouraged me to ponder on His timeless teachings. The gentle breeze reminded me of the many souls who once gathered here seeking hope and understanding.

The Sermon on the Mount: A Reflection on the Beatitudes

In the Sermon on the Mount, Jesus shared an important message. This message includes the Beatitudes, which are found in Matthew 5 to 7 of his Gospel. These teachings resonate deeply with millions of Christians around the world today. It's inspiring that these ancient words still guide and uplift many lives today.

The Beatitudes express key teachings of Jesus. An example is, *"Blessed are the poor in spirit, for theirs is the kingdom of heaven."* Another example is *"Blessed are the peacemakers, for they shall be called children of God."* They convey a profound message of hope, compassion, and humility. Standing in the very place where these words were spoken deepened my understanding of Christ's transforming messages.

I reflected on these teachings. I felt a deep connection to the many seekers of truth. They have been inspired by them throughout the years.

It is through embodying these principles that we can truly create a more loving and just world for all.

Exploring the Mount of Beatitudes Church

The beautiful Church of the Beatitudes stands at the center of the Mount of Beatitudes. Italian architect Antonio Barluzzi designed it in 1930. This church boasts an elegant yet understated design, characterized by its octagonal shape, symbolizing each of the Beatitudes. The serene gardens offer a peaceful sanctuary for worshipers to pray and meditate.

Upon entering the church, I was instantly enveloped by a profound sense of reverence. The serene ambiance, merged with the gentle natural light pouring through the windows, provided the perfect setting for reflective prayer. Its location near Galilee allows visitors to see the lands where Jesus taught and lived.

The historical significance of this area adds an extra layer of meaning to the spiritual experience. Walking through the archway, I felt a deep sense of history. The echoes of countless prayers have been said in these sacred walls over the years.

Spiritual Reflection and Personal Connection

The Mount of Beatitudes serves as a profound testament to Jesus' ministry, offering an exceptional setting for contemplation and prayer. Set in peaceful surroundings, this location invites profound reflection. It is rich in spiritual meaning and ideal for sincere communication with the divine.

Visiting the Mount of Beatitudes was more than just a historical or religious experience. It provided a deep opportunity for personal spiritual reflection. Sitting on the hillside, I appreciated Jesus' teachings on humility, mercy, and peace, finding them highly relevant today. Those words echoed deeply within me, leaving a lasting impact.

The stunning natural beauty deepens this profound connection. Surrounded by olive trees and wildflowers, I easily focused on my faith, free from distractions. The Mount of Beatitudes is a place for those seeking to enhance their spiritual journey and better understand Christ's teachings.

A Pilgrim's Journey

A visit to the Mount of Beatitudes should be an essential part of every pilgrim's journey. This sacred site strengthens my connection to biblical history. It aids spiritual growth. It leaves me with a deep sense of peace. I came away with a renewed appreciation for Jesus' simple yet powerful message.

The Mount of Beatitudes highlights that God's kingdom is based on humility, kindness, and compassion, not power or wealth. Pilgrims visit this sacred site to think about their faith and strengthen their connection to Christ's teachings.

I stood on the mount, surrounded by a beautiful landscape. I felt deep gratitude for the chance to walk in such special places. This experience has motivated me to practice love and compassion in my daily life.

Conclusion: Discovering Peace on the Mount of Beatitudes

My visit to the Mount of Beatitudes was truly unforgettable. The site's stunning beauty captivated me. Its historical importance and spiritual significance make it one of the most remarkable places I've visited in Israel. Pilgrims and travelers alike should experience the serene peacefulness of the Mount of Beatitudes. This allows them to connect with Jesus' teachings and appreciate its rich heritage. It is a destination that promises a peaceful and transforming experience.

My experience has highlighted the important lessons of the Beatitudes, encouraging me to live with compassion, humility, and peace. This place will forever resonate in my heart as a beacon of Christ's transforming message of hope and love.

I walked through the gardens. I felt a deep connection to the centuries of faith that have thrived in this place. Each moment spent in this sacred space deepened my understanding of spirituality and the universal wish for inner peace.

The wayward son

He took his share, with restless heart,
And from his father' s home did part.
With dreams of freedom, far and wide,
He journeyed forth with foolish pride.

The world was vast, its pleasures sweet,
And in its arms, he lost his feet.
He squandered all, his fortune gone,
And found himself alone, withdrawn.

A famine struck, the land grew bare,
And none were left to help or care.
In desperate straits, he fed the swine,
While longing for what once was mine.

How many servants in my home,
He thought, would never be alone?
I' ll rise and go, and to him say,
Father, I' ve sinned and lost my way.

With humble heart and weary stride,
He made the journey back, his pride
denied.
But far away, his father' s eyes
Saw him and ran, his voice a cry

My son has come, once dead, now found!

Bring robes and rings, let joy abound!
Prepare a feast, for this my son
Was lost but now his journey' s done.

www.drandrewcskoh.com

Mount of Beatitudes

CHURCH OF
BEATITUDES ON
MOUNT OF
BEATITUDES,
SITE WHERE
JESUS
DELIVERED HIS
SERMON ON THE
MOUNT,
MATTHEW 5: 3-16

Chapter 18
Church of the Nativity: Birthplace of Jesus

Church of Nativity

Take a trip to Bethlehem and experience the Church of the Nativity, the believed birthplace of Jesus Christ. This enlightening visit offers a profound understanding of the church's historical, spiritual, and religious importance, ensuring an unforgettable experience.

My visit to the Church of the Nativity in Bethlehem, the recognized birthplace of Jesus Christ, was profoundly moving. This historic site provides a unique insight into the Christian faith. It allows me to connect with the early life of the Savior.

Stepping Into Jesus' Birthplace

The Church of the Nativity in Bethlehem is a very important place for Christians. It is believed that this is the place where Jesus Christ was born. Visiting this ancient church was truly inspirational! For centuries pilgrims have visited this humble yet spiritual site in search of strength.

As I wandered through the dimly lit chambers, the atmosphere was thick with reverence and history. The flickering candles whispered stories of faith, reminding me of the many souls who had come here before.

Arriving in Bethlehem

Bethlehem, located a mere stone's throw from Jerusalem, is an ancient biblical city brimming with profound spiritual significance. As I neared Bethlehem, I felt a surreal sense of wonder. Spirituality filled me. I realized I was about to visit the birthplace of Jesus at Manger Square. This is the home of the Church of the Nativity.

Upon entering this church, the weight of its historic and religious significance is instantly clear. The church was established by Constantine the Great in 327 AD. It is the oldest continuously operating church in the world. It was transformed into its current form in the 6th century AD.

Entering the Church of the Nativity

Upon entering this church, I was captivated by its profound simplicity and sense of reverence. The interior features early Christian and Byzantine architecture. Columns and mosaics highlight its history. They foster a peaceful environment for reflection and worship.

The dim lighting creates a solemn atmosphere. Slender windows let in soft golden rays. These rays warm the ancient stone walls. Even in the midst of a bustling crowd, a profound sense of peace prevails.

As I explored the sanctuary, I felt surrounded by its history, with each stone telling stories from long ago. I felt a connection to those who had visited this sacred space before, seeking comfort and spiritual support.

The Nativity Grotto

Entering the Nativity Grotto was a definite highlight of my visit. It is the sacred place thought to be where Jesus was born. Descending the narrow staircase, I was enveloped by a profound sense of awe. I stood in the sacred spot marked by a silver star, where Christ's birth took place.

Kneeling to touch the cool stone filled me with reverence for this significant moment. Touching the silver star at His birthplace reminded me of His humble beginnings and the core of His ministry.

The flickering candles cast a warm glow, illuminating the faces of fellow pilgrims who shared in this unforgettable experience.

Kneeling at this sacred site was a profoundly moving experience. The unpretentious environment felt fitting for commemorating the place where our Savior first came into the world. Softly flickering candles illuminated the space, while pilgrims offered their prayers in quiet reverence.

Exploring the Church Complex

Besides the Nativity Grotto, the Church of the Nativity complex includes other important historical and spiritual sites to visit. One such site is the Chapel of the Manger, where Mary was believed to have placed Jesus after His birth. This offers another opportunity for reflection and prayer.

Nearby attractions include notable churches. One example is the Roman Catholic Church of Saint Catherine. It holds a captivating midnight Mass tradition on Christmas Eve. This church, with its modern design, still exudes unique beauty and is important within the Nativity complex.

Spiritual Reflections on the Birth of Christ

I visited the Church of the Nativity. It helped me feel a strong personal connection to the story of Christ's birth. Being in the very place where this miraculous event occurred infused the narrative with a profound depth and significance.

Reflecting on Christ's humble birth in a stable rather than a palace highlights His messages of simplicity, love, and grace. This experience has not only deepened my Christian faith but also revitalized my spirit and renewed my sense of purpose.

I stood in the quiet of the church. I felt a sense of peace wash over me. It reminded me of the importance of hope and faith in our lives. Each flickering candle illuminated the path of devotion, symbolizing the light Christ brought into the world.

Historical and Religious Significance

The Church of the Nativity is more than an important site; it signifies the ongoing and challenging history of Christianity. Spanning centuries of conflict, transformation, and revival, its rich legacy shines as a beacon of faith and hope. Established by Constantine and designated a UNESCO World Heritage Site, its significance endures through time.

For Christians, visiting the Church of the Nativity is more than a pilgrimage. It signifies a deep return to the roots of their faith. This historic site acts as a bridge between contemporary believers and the birthplace of Jesus, cultivating a deeply personal experience.

Conclusion: A Pilgrimage to Remember

My pilgrimage to the Church of the Nativity was an overwhelmingly spiritual and transforming experience. Praying in the Nativity Grotto deepened my understanding of Jesus' timeless message. Exploring its ancient halls enriched this understanding of hope, peace, and love. This message has profoundly shaped history.

Every Christian traveler and pilgrim must make a pilgrimage to the Church of the Nativity when visiting the Holy Land. This sacred site inspires visitors to think about Christ's miraculous birth and the lasting message of His life and sacrifice.

The reverence and peace found within its walls serve as a reminder of the enduring faith that transcends generations. Ultimately, this pilgrimage not only enriches the soul but also strengthens one's connection to the global Christian community.

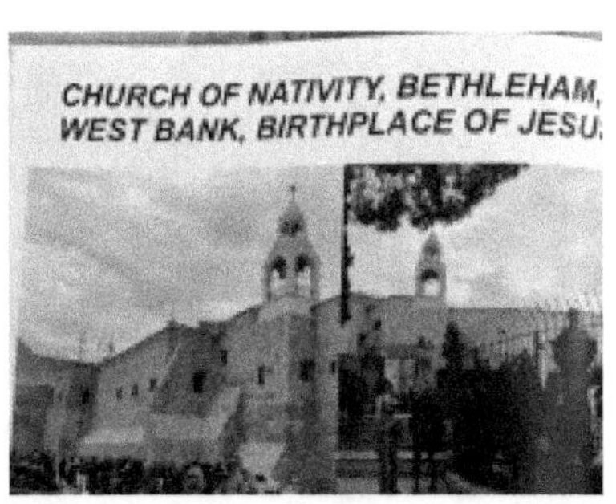

Chapter 19
Pool of Bethesda Pool: Healing Power

Bethesda

Explore the Pool of Bethesda, where Jesus healed a paralyzed man. Examine its biblical, historical and spiritual significance during a personal account of visiting this holy site in Jerusalem.

Visiting the Bethesda Pool in Jerusalem was an exhilarating journey through biblical history. This is a historic site where Jesus is said to have healed people. Being there made the powerful story of healing come to life, offering a profound opportunity for reflection and spiritual renewal.

Lion Gate

The Pool of Bethesda, located near Lion's Gate (St Stephen's Gate) in Jerusalem, is steeped in profound biblical significance. This site, mentioned in the Gospel of John for Jesus healing a paralyzed man, continues to inspire Christians worldwide. During my visit, I was fortunate enough to experience its captivating beauty and rich history firsthand.

Biblical Significance

The Pool of Bethesda holds a significant place in the Christian faith. John 5:1-15 describes a sacred site known for its miraculous healing powers. The healing was believed to be activated when an angel occasionally stirred the waters. Those who entered afterward were instantly healed. At this significant spot, Jesus met a paralyzed man who had suffered for 38 years. He told the man, "Get up, take your bed, and walk." This command led to an immediate healing.

As I prepared to visit this sacred site, the theme of healing resonated deeply with Christians. It symbolizes both physical and spiritual renewal. I realized I would be standing on the ground of a remarkable divine intervention. My awe grew immensely.

The historical and spiritual weight of Bethesda engulfed me, prompting reflections on faith and the transforming power of belief. Each step toward the pool felt like a journey through time and into my understanding of hope and redemption.

Arriving at Bethesda Pool

The Pool of Bethesda is in the Muslim Quarter of Jerusalem, near St. Anne Church, and I was instantly captivated by its peaceful vibe. This peaceful archaeological park offers a glimpse into the area's rich history and made for a delightful visit.

The remains of this grand pool are vast and deep, with ancient stone steps leading into it. It's easy to imagine crowds gathering here, drawn by the promise of healing. The palpable history of the site invites moments of tranquil reflection on the miracles of the past.

As I walked along the edges, I couldn't help but admire the intricate mosaics that still tell stories of old. The serenity of the place and the gentle sound of water, created a soothing atmosphere that felt almost sacred.

An Exploration Through History: Archaeological Importance

The Pool of Bethesda has been carefully excavated and restored, but its rich history remains visible in its ancient stones. This site features remains from the Roman and Byzantine periods. It was part of a network of water reservoirs in Jerusalem, which supplied water to cities and temples. While its original purpose centered on water provision, it gradually embraced profound religious significance over the centuries.

When I explored the area, I learned that this pool was once divided into two reservoirs. Colonnades and structures, which connected the reservoirs, still exist. Archaeologists have discovered the remains of five porches mentioned in the Gospel of John. This gives visitors like me a clear view of the area's layout during biblical times.

Spiritual Reflection

Standing by the timeless waters of Bethesda's Pool, I was deeply moved by its remarkable history. Jesus healing a paralyzed man demonstrates His compassion, mercy, and divine power. This event highlights a powerful example of both physical and spiritual healing. Such healing is accessible to everyone. When Jesus asked, "Do you want to be made well?" it was an invitation for anyone seeking healing in body, mind, or spirit.

At the Bethesda Pool, I prayed, reflecting on God's healing power throughout history and today. Being at such a significant location where Jesus walked and performed miracles profoundly touched me. It reminds me that faith is timeless and Jesus' healing power is still relevant today.

St. Anne Church

Next to the Pool of Bethesda is St. Anne Church, a beautiful Romanesque-style church dedicated to St Anne, the mother of Virgin Mary. I was captivated by the beautiful acoustics and the harmonious singing of pilgrims, which echoed off the stone walls. This created an undeniably spiritual and uplifting atmosphere, making my visit truly unforgettable!

The Church of St. Anne combines simplicity and elegance with beautiful stone arches and a serene interior perfect for reflection. While wandering the church, I felt a strong connection to its history and faith. Each corner held whispers of prayers and the sacred moments shared by countless visitors over the centuries.

Legacy of Bethesda Pool

The Pool of Bethesda continues to enchant visitors from around the world. Its inspiring narrative of hope, healing, and transformation captivates many. Christians often visit Bethesda for religious purposes or personal reflection. Its rich legacy connects them to the ministry and miracles of Jesus. It profoundly reminds us of faith's essential role. Faith guides our individual paths toward wholeness and healing.

Upon departing from Bethesda, I was enveloped by an immediate feeling of peace and spiritual rejuvenation. Walking through this sacred, time-honored site was deeply inspiring. The faith at this place was rich. The miracles happened there illuminated the profound healing and restoration that trust in God can offer.

Conclusion: An Adventure to Remember

Visiting the Pool of Bethesda was a profoundly inspiring experience. It invites visitors to contemplate its enduring messages of faith, hope, and restoration. I stood among its ruins. I felt a deep connection to the biblical stories. Many pilgrims have journeyed here before me.

Travelers exploring the Holy Land should definitely include a visit to the Bethesda Pool in their itinerary. This remarkable site offers a glimpse into ancient history. It also serves as a poignant opportunity to contemplate healing and faith today.

The Road to Jericho

Upon the road to Jericho,
A traveler walked with steps so slow.
But thieves lay wait in shadows deep,
To strike and leave him there to weep.

They beat him down, they stripped him bare,
And left him in despair's cold snare.
The road was silent, none to hear,
His groans of pain, his cries of fear.

A priest then came, in robes of white,
He saw the man, then turned from sight.
A Levite next, with holy tread,
Looked once, then hurried on instead.

But then a stranger, foreign, low,
A Samaritan, his heart aglow,
Beheld the man with tender eyes,
And in his chest, compassion rise.

He knelt beside the broken form,
His hands brought healing, soft and warm.
With oil and wine, his wounds were bound,
Then gently raised him from the ground.

He placed him on a donkey's back,
And led him down the winding track.
An inn they found, a place to stay,
Where safety, care, and rest could lay.

The stranger paid with silver coin,
Ensuring care, no need to join.
Whatever more this man may need,
I'll cover it, his life to feed.

So who, dear friend, is neighbor true?
The one who shows what love can do.
For in this tale, we learn and see,
True mercy knows no boundary.

www.drandrewcskoh.com/poems

Chapter 20
Mount Nebo: Bronze Serpent Monument

Bronze Serpent

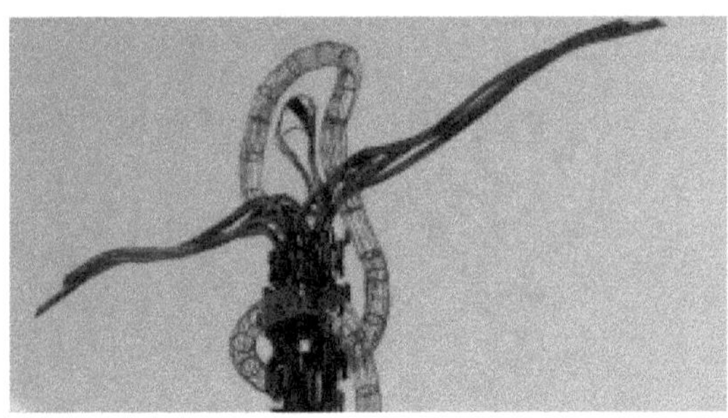

Explore the spiritual and historical significance of Jordan's Bronze Serpent Monument. Discover its Biblical roots, connections with Moses, and stunning location atop Mount Nebo.

My visit to the Bronze Serpent Monument on Mount Nebo was an inspiring journey through biblical history. This symbolic monument evokes the story of Moses and God's healing and deliverance. Perched high above the Promised Land, it offered not only breathtaking views but also deep opportunities for reflection.

Bronze Serpent Monument

Located on Mount Nebo in Jordan, the Bronze Serpent Monument symbolizes healing, faith, and biblical history. This impressive sculpture, connected to the stories of Moses and the Israelites, is a popular pilgrimage site. During my visit, I was inspired by its deep meaning and the stunning views of the Promised Land.

Biblical Story

The Bronze Serpent Monument is inspired by a powerful story from the Old Testament, specifically Numbers 21:4-9. As the Israelites journeyed through the wilderness, many fell ill due to their disobedience. In response to their plight, God commanded Moses to fashion a bronze serpent and raise it on a pole. Those who gazed upon this emblem experienced immediate healing, symbolizing God's mercy and provision for His people.

This narrative suggests the New Testament message of salvation, where Jesus compares Himself to a bronze serpent (John 3:14-15). Today, this monument serves as a poignant reminder of God's past healing and the ultimate restoration offered through Christ.

Arriving at Mount Nebo

Mount Nebo is an important biblical site. According to the Bible, Moses saw the Promised Land for the last time here. This occurred before he died. I climbed the winding roads to the top. I felt a deep sense of historical importance. The sacred site also gave me a feeling of spiritual importance. The panoramic vistas overlooking the Jordan Valley, the Dead Sea, and even Jerusalem on clear days are simply breathtaking!

As I drew nearer to the monument, its captivating design captivated me. Italian artist Giovanni Fantoni created this striking sculpture of the bronze serpent. It is wrapped around a cross-like pole. This symbolizes the fulfillment of Old Testament prophecy in the New Testament.

Exploring the Bronze Serpent Monument

The Bronze Serpent Monument boasts a design that is both striking and deeply meaningful. The monument invites visitors to think about its significance in biblical stories, particularly in The Book of Numbers.

Standing before this monument transported me to the heart of Israel's journey, rich with lessons in trust and faith. Being at Mount Nebo, where Moses spent his final moments, was deeply humbling. It was also a powerful reminder of a significant biblical story. Here, Moses gazed upon the land promised to his descendants, a legacy established long after Abraham's passing.

Memorial Church of Moses

Visiting the Bronze Serpent Monument at Mount Nebo was not just a historical exploration; it was a profound spiritual experience. Looking out at the breathtaking landscape that Moses once saw, I felt awed by God's faithfulness and provision. Standing there, the profound messages of healing and hope resonated with me in an incredibly tangible way.

Mount Nebo is a serene place for prayer and contemplation. It is known for its beautiful mosaics. The simple stone structures foster personal devotion to God. The Memorial Church of Moses significantly enriches this sacred experience. The harmonious blend of beautiful mosaics and tranquil surroundings provides serene spaces for peaceful contemplation.

A Scenic View of the Promised Land

Mount Nebo offers a breathtaking view that spans miles. It showcases the beautiful landscapes of Jordan and the Jordan River. On clear days, you can even see the far-off cities of Jerusalem and Bethlehem. I discovered that the lookout points near its monument are perfect for fully embracing this magnificent panorama.

My perspective brought a profound sense of personal reflection and inspiration. Moses, after years of leading his people, stands at the wilderness's edge and catches a glimpse of the Promised Land. This moment is both powerful and motivational. This strong imagery reminds me to trust God's timing while developing perseverance and faith.

Legacy

Mount Nebo's rich history has made it a popular pilgrimage destination. It attracts not only Christians but also diverse visitors seeking a spiritual connection to biblical history. Pilgrims come to pay tribute to Moses and contemplate Israel's wilderness journey. This serene environment provides a tranquil space for deep reflection on life, faith, and the promises of God.

Travelers to Jordan in search of an extraordinary experience should not miss the Bronze Serpent Monument. This site is full of biblical importance and offers stunning views of Mount Nebo. It promises an enriching experience for pilgrims, history enthusiasts, or those seeking inspiration.

Conclusion: An Experience to Remember

Visiting the Bronze Serpent Monument at Mount Nebo was a profoundly emotional and intellectually enriching experience. Standing where Moses once stood, I felt a deep connection to the biblical and historical significance of the Promised Land. This visit became a powerful, unforgettable reminder of faith, healing, and hope in my life.

Mount Nebo and the Bronze Serpent Monument in Jordan offer a unique opportunity. Visitors can explore history and meditate on its lasting lessons.

Looking out at the vast landscape below, I felt a sense of peace that calmed my thoughts and encouraged reflection. Every moment here highlights the lasting strength of belief and our search for understanding and purpose.

The Parable of the Sower

A sower went out with seeds to sow,
Casting them wide, wherever they'd go.
Some fell on the path, hard and dry,
Snatched by the birds that flew in the
sky.

Some seeds fell on rocky ground,They
sprang up quick, but roots weren't
found.Under the sun, they withered
away,No depth to grow, no place to stay.

Others fell among the thorns,Choked by
the weeds as they were born.The
worries of life, riches, and pride,
Smothered their growth, though they
tried.

But some seeds fell on fertile soil,Deep
in the earth, where none could spoil.
They grew strong, tall, with fruitful yield,
A hundredfold harvest, the richest field.

He who has ears, let him hear,The
message is simple, the meaning is clear:
The Word is the seed, the soil is the
heart,Receive it with faith, and let it take
part.

Prepare the soul, clear the ground,Let
the Word take root, and fruit abound.In
patience and love, let it grow,In the
harvest, the life will show.

www.drandrewcskoh.com

BRONZE
SERPENT
MT NEBO WHERE MOSES WAS GRANTED A VIEW OF THE PROMISED LAND

MISED LAND

Chapter 21

Hezekiah's Tunnel and Pool of Siloam: Ancient Wonders of Jerusalem

Hezekiah's Tunnel

Discover the amazing history of Hezekiah's Tunnel and the Pool of Siloam through personal stories and ancient engineering.

Visiting Hezekiah's Tunnel and the Pool of Siloam in Jerusalem was an amazing experience. It took me back thousands of years to the heart of antiquity. While exploring the water passageway built by King Hezekiah, I felt a deep connection to the biblical era. I was amazed by the incredible engineering of the ancient world when I reached the Siloam Pool.

Hezekiah's Tunnel and Siloam Pool

Jerusalem is a remarkable city, brimming with history, faith, and extraordinary examples of ancient engineering. A highlight of my trip was exploring Hezekiah's Tunnel. The Pool of Siloam also stands out. These sites exemplify remarkable engineering and have deep biblical importance.

I walked through Hezekiah's Tunnel, designed to protect Jerusalem's water supply. I felt a strong connection to history. It was as if the past was alive beneath my feet. The dark passage echoed with the sound of dripping water, a reminder of the many lives depending on it. At the Pool of Siloam, I was enchanted by its serene beauty and the stories hidden in its waters.

The History of Hezekiah's Tunnel

Hezekiah's Tunnel is also known as Siloam Tunnel. It is an impressive ancient engineering project built around 701 BC. This was during King Hezekiah's reign. It served as a strategic defense against the Assyrian siege.

Hezekiah cleverly directed the waters of Gihon Spring into Jerusalem via an underground channel. This provided a steady water supply for the city's residents. This occurred even during wartime, as detailed in 2 Kings 20:20 and 2 Chronicles 32:30.

The tunnel is 1,750 feet long and was dug from both ends by two teams that met in the middle. The remarkable ingenuity and precision displayed by ancient civilizations was nothing short of miraculous.

Walking through the dimly lit passage, I could almost hear the echoes of those who had traversed it centuries ago. The cool water flowing through the tunnel highlights how crucial this engineering feat was for Jerusalem's survival.

Walking Through Hezekiah's Tunnel

Exploring Hezekiah's Tunnel was an amazing experience. The water from Gihon Spring varied in height. At times, it reached my ankles, and at other times, it reached my knees! The tunnel's narrow, low passages forced me to stoop, enhancing the thrill of the adventure.

Cool water flowed gently. Footsteps echoed against the ancient walls. An air of mystery created an unforgettable atmosphere. It was reminiscent of Jerusalem's struggles during an impending siege. I couldn't help thinking back on biblical accounts which mentioned this same tunnel connecting past to present in tangible terms.

A Biblical Healing Site

At the end of a tunnel lies the Pool of Siloam, a significant biblical site. In John 9:1-12, Jesus heals a blind man. He makes a paste with His saliva and applies it to the man's eyes. Then, Jesus tells him to wash in the pool of Siloam. Many pilgrims are attracted to the miracles at Siloam. They seek to connect with its rich history and spiritual importance. This remarkable act is a key attraction today.

This pool, an integral part of Jerusalem's ancient water system, sourced its water from Hezekiah's Tunnel. During my visit, I was captivated by its unadorned beauty; its profound historical importance imparted a sense of reverence.

Excavation is underway at a nearby site. The goal is to gain more insights into the City of David. The pool played an important role in the lives of its residents.

Spiritual and Historical Significance

My visit to Hezekiah's Tunnel and the Pool of Siloam transcended mere historical exploration; it was a profoundly spiritual journey. I walked through King Hezekiah's underground passage. This passage was meant to protect his people. I also stood near the place where Jesus performed miracles. These experiences filled me with deep emotion and inspiration. These locations bring the events in scripture to life, making them more meaningful than just reading about them.

The tunnel and pool stand as powerful symbols of God's provision and protection throughout history. King Hezekiah demonstrated faith in God by strengthening his city for battle. Centuries later, Jesus used the Pool of Siloam to reveal God's healing power. Visiting these incredible sites strengthened my faith and enhanced my understanding of familiar biblical stories.

Practical Tips for Exploring Hezekiah's Tunnel and Pool of Siloam
Here are a few practical tips on visiting these two landmarks:
Prepare for water

To guarantee your safety while exploring a water-filled tunnel, wear water-friendly shoes. Choose clothing that can be easily rolled up, like shorts or lightweight pants.

Bring a flashlight

Some parts of the tunnel are lit. An extra light source like a flashlight or headlamp is very helpful in the darker areas.

Be mindful of the space

Tunnels can feel tight and cramped, so if you're afraid of small spaces or feel uneasy, be careful.

Visit Early

To fully enjoy your experience, arriving early is highly recommended. This creates a peaceful visit and offers a great chance for reflection at the Pool of Siloam afterward.

Conclusion: An Excursion Through Faith and History

My visit to Hezekiah's Tunnel and the Pool of Siloam was a meaningful experience, connecting ancient history with spiritual importance. Walking through the tunnel was enlightening. Standing at the site of Jesus's miracles deepened my biblical understanding. It also offered new insights into my faith.

Hezekiah's Tunnel and the Pool of Siloam in Jerusalem are must-see destinations for anyone exploring the city. These remarkable sites offer a fascinating look into history and remind us of God's constant presence throughout time.

These iconic landmarks are perfect for pilgrims and history lovers. They are also ideal for anyone wanting to connect with biblical stories. The landmarks guarantee a memorable experience for all visitors.

Hezekiah's Tunnel and the Pool of Siloam will deeply impact you.

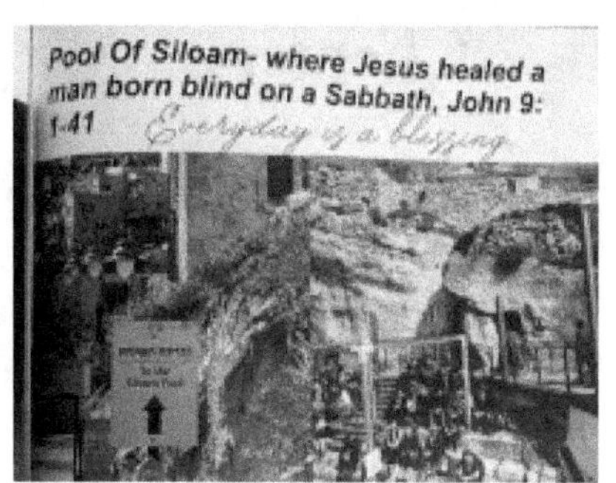
Pool Of Siloam- where Jesus healed a
man born blind on a Sabbath, John 9:
1-41
Everyday is a blessing

Chapter 22
City of David: Journey Through Biblical History

City of David

Take an exciting walk through the City of David, where the history and spirituality of Jerusalem come to life. Explore ancient ruins, delve into the legacy of King David, and witness iconic biblical landmarks on this unforgettable adventure!

Visiting the City of David in Jerusalem was an incredible experience. Ancient artifacts, biblical stories, and King David's legacy came together in one of the world's best archaeological sites. Strolling through the historic streets enriched my connection to both faith and history, laying a strong foundation for my experience.

Uncovering Jerusalem's Ancient Roots

Jerusalem is a city full of history and spirit. A great way to explore its heritage is by visiting the City of David. This site is seen as the ancient heart of Jerusalem over 3,000 years ago. Exploring this site was a historical journey. It was also a spiritual awakening. King David established his kingdom here. Many biblical events took place in this area.

Historical Significance

The City of David is more than merely an archaeological site; it is the cornerstone of contemporary Jerusalem. This historic area is located just outside the Old City walls. It became Jerusalem's capital under King David, as detailed in 2 Samuel 5:6-10. Today, it is filled with ancient artifacts. These artifacts showcase its transformation from Canaanite origins to its importance in the Israeli monarchy.

Exploring the City of David was incredible. The experience connected me to its biblical past. This past has shaped Israel's history. It's astonishing that this site, with its ruins and winding passages, was where David ruled. He was a key figure in the Bible and lived here.

Key Sites in the City of David

My visit to the City of David revealed important archaeological finds that bring Biblical stories to life. Some standout moments from my exploration included:

Gihon Spring

The Gihon Spring, one of the most ancient water sources in Jerusalem, played a crucial role in the city's survival. It is famously known as the site where King Solomon was anointed as king, as described in 1 Kings 1:33-39. I stood by this historic spring. I imagined the grand ceremonies. Royal events took place here thousands of years ago. History surrounded me. It stirred my imagination with echoes of ancient rituals. This sacred site held great importance.

Hezekiah's Tunnel

Constructed during the reign of King Hezekiah, this remarkable engineering achievement is a highlight of the City of David. I walked through this ancient tunnel. It was carved to protect Jerusalem's water source from the Assyrians (2 Chronicles 20:20). This experience gave me a deep appreciation for history and resilience.

Archaeologists are confident they have uncovered the remnants of King David's palace in this very location. Standing here, I could envision David himself overlooking his city, contemplating pivotal decisions that would shape the future of Israel.

The Pool of Siloam is located at the terminus of Hezekiah's Tunnel. It is renowned as the site where Jesus performed a remarkable healing miracle (John 9:1-11). Visiting this sacred pool allowed me to feel a profound connection between the events of the Old and New Testaments.

Spiritual Impact of Visiting the City of David

While wandering through the City of David, I was profoundly moved by its spiritual significance. King David wrote many Psalms in this sacred place. God made His covenant with Israel here, marking the country's rich history.

Jerusalem stood out during my visit. I felt its enduring presence as a symbol of faith, hope, and resilience for thousands of years. I stood on the stones once walked by ancient Israelites. I felt a deep connection to their lasting faith. This faith inspires millions worldwide.

Archaeological Discoveries

The City of David has recently become a key site for important archaeological digs. These digs reveal amazing finds that illuminate its rich history. An extensive underground tunnel system that once functioned as a crucial water storage facility has been discovered. Recent excavations have uncovered ancient homes, streets, and structures, offering valuable insights into the daily lives of early Jerusalem residents. Visiting these archaeological sites felt like stepping back in time, allowing me to see where Biblical figures once lived.

A recent exciting discovery is the Large Stone Structure, which some researchers believe might have been King David's palace. More evidence is needed. Yet, this discovery highlights Jerusalem's rich ancient history. It also deepens our understanding of the City of David.

Practical Information for Exploring the City of David

Wear comfortable shoes

The terrain can be uneven, and you'll likely do quite a lot of walking.

Prepare for Hezekiah's Tunnel

If you plan to walk through Hezekiah's Tunnel, bring water shoes and a flashlight. It's an amazing adventure that involves walking through shallow water!

Take a guided tour

To avoid crowds and maximize peace, consider booking a guided tour at The City of David.

Visit early

To avoid the crowds, arriving early in the day will give you a more serene experience.

Conclusion: Deep Encounter with Jerusalem's Biblical Past

My visit to the City of David changed my perspective. It helped me better understand Jerusalem's ancient roots. I also gained insight into its biblical history. As I wandered through this historic site, the stories of Biblical events and figures were vividly brought to life. It is more than an archaeological site; it is a vibrant testament to Jerusalem's important role in history and faith.

The City of David is a must-visit destination for anyone traveling to Jerusalem. This impressive site seamlessly combines history and modernity, letting visitors experience the rich legacy of kings, prophets, and pilgrims. No matter what your interest is, there is something inspiring for you here!

The Parable of the Mustard Seed

A seed so small, within the hand,
Unnoticed in the fertile land,
Yet buried deep, its roots take hold,

A secret tale the soil has told.

The earth is stirred, the skies agree,

A promise wrapped in mystery.
Through sun and storm, it finds its
way,
From darkness into light of day.

And as it grows, the birds will sing,
The seed becomes a mighty thing.
A tree that shelters, wide and
grand,
A haven in the heart of land.

So too, the kingdom starts so small,

A whisper, nearly missed by all,
But with its roots in truth and grace,

It blossoms wide, fills every space.

The smallest faith, like mustard
seed,
Can move the mountains, meet the
need.
For in the smallest, lies the grand,
In tiny things, God's mighty hand.

www.drandrewcskoh.com/poems

Chapter 23
Yad Hashmona Biblical Garden: Seder Meal

Biblical Garden

Experience biblical history at Yad Hashmona Biblical Garden. Enjoy a traditional Seder meal. Connect with ancient customs and Israel's spiritual heritage.

I traveled to the Yad Hashmona Biblical Garden. This trip gave me a personal look into biblical history. It provided a hands-on experience that brought scripture alive. The elegant Seder meal deepened my understanding of ancient Israeli customs and their enduring importance.

Navigating Through Biblical Times

On my trip to Israel, I visited Yad Hashmona Biblical Garden. It is an exquisitely designed space that brings biblical times alive! Located in the stunning Judean Hills, this garden allows visitors to connect with biblical history and traditions. My visit ended with an immersive Seder meal. It deepened my understanding of Jewish customs. It connected me to the rich spiritual heritage of this vibrant culture.

Exploring the Yad Hashmona Biblical Garden

The Yad Hashmona Biblical Garden invites visitors to immerse themselves in the rich tapestry of biblical agriculture, culture, and spirituality. I was thrilled to discover plants, ancient tools, and structures. They reminded me of biblical times. These elements brought the customs of those people to life and made the scripture feel real. Each part of this beautiful garden held symbolic meaning, vividly bringing its Scriptures to life.

Key features of the garden were:

Terraced agriculture

Seeing how ancient Israelites farmed on hills made me think about the hard work they needed to grow food. It also required faith to cultivate in tough conditions.

Wine and olive presses were important ancient tools. They showed the significance of vineyards and olive groves in daily life. These tools also played a role in spiritual practices in Israel.

Biblical Plants and Trees

During my exploration of Biblical plants and trees, I discovered fig trees, date palms, and pomegranates. These plants are all named in scripture with special meanings.

Wandering through the garden felt like stepping into ancient Israel, full of vibrant customs and traditions. My comprehension of their daily lives and practices deepened remarkably with each step I took.

The Seder Meal: A Rich Tradition of Faith and Freedom

After exploring the garden, we gathered for a traditional Seder meal, a key part of the Jewish Passover celebrations. This meaningful feast honored Israel's exodus from Egypt through symbolic foods and rituals that narrate the powerful story of liberation. As a Christian, this experience also deepened my understanding of the Last Supper that Jesus shared with His disciples.

At dinner, our guide explained the significance of each element for both Passover and our faith journeys.

Key components of a Seder meal include:

Matzah (unleavened bread)

The unleavened bread symbolizes the essence of freedom and rapid redemption, recalling the Israelites' rapid escape from Egypt. In contrast, the bitter herbs, powerfully evokes the suffering and anguish experienced during their enslavement before liberation.

Haroset, a sweet mixture of fruits, was utilized by the Israelites in Egypt as a mortar for construction. This delightful blend offered a striking contrast to their bitterness, symbolizing the hope of redemption.

Four cups of wine

Each glass symbolized one of God's four promises to free His people and added joy to the meal.

Participating in the Seder meal was an inspiring experience that helped me connect with Israel's rich traditions. Participating deepened my appreciation for the rituals Jesus observed, enhancing my personal connection to the biblical stories I've learned.

Spiritual Reflections

My experience at the Yad Hashmona Biblical Garden and Seder meal inspired deep spiritual insights. The experience connected Scripture, history, and faith in a tangible way. Observing Israel's customs through a biblical lens deepened the meaning of familiar passages.

Key takeaways

Living Scripture

The garden offered a glimpse into the physical world of Scripture. It made its stories more tangible for visitors. Every plant, tool, and structure symbolized God's care for His people, reflecting His presence in their daily lives.

Experience the Seder

The Seder meal served as a powerful reminder of God's ongoing care and faithfulness throughout history. Each element of this symbolic feast enriched my understanding of His plan for the redemption of humanity.

Connection to Jesus' Time

Jesus followed these customs, which helped me understand more about faith and tradition today. This gives more context for New Testament stories. Tips for Visiting Yad Hashmona Biblical Garden

Tips for Visiting Yad Hashmona Biblical Garden

Here are some simple tips to enhance your visit to Yad Hashmona Biblical Garden:

Dress appropriately

Wear comfortable shoes and bring sunscreen or a hat to prevent sunburns

Take your time

This garden showcases detailed copies of plants from the Bible, offering many chances to stop and ponder on their meanings.

Join in a Seder meal

Try to join a Seder meal during your visit to deepen the experience of biblical stories!

Conclusion: A Spiritual Journey Into Biblical Times

Exploring the Yad Hashmona Biblical Garden was a profound and enlightening experience, offering deep historical context and rich spiritual reflections. Participating in a Seder meal strengthened my connection to Jewish and my own faith traditions. Visiting Yad Hashmona was a unique experience that reveals timeless truths in new ways.

JAD HASOMA BIBLICAL GARDEN

Epilogue

As my journey ended, I came back from Israel with cherished memories, a strengthened faith, a new sense of purpose, and a feeling of His presence all around me and within myself as well. Holy sites have evolved from distant biblical locations to meaningful symbols of God's presence in my life and the world.

Every place I explored, from Galilee to Mount Carmel, enriched my appreciation for God's unwavering love and faithfulness. Pilgrimage is not just about reaching a physical destination; it's a deep personal journey where we invite Christ to be with us.

Upon returning home, I felt a profound urge to share my experience with others. My goal is to inspire readers to explore the scriptures anew, experience the Holy Land, and embark on their own spiritual journeys, whether through travel or daily faith practices.

While my pilgrimage has come to a close, my journey with Christ is just beginning. May His presence illuminate your path, drawing you ever closer to His heart.

One Last Thing

Thank you for selecting my book. I genuinely hope it has offered you an enjoyable and stimulating experience. I would appreciate your feedback and would be grateful if you could write a review on the platform where you bought it or on a book review site. Your feedback will help others make choices and show me which parts of the book were effective or lacking. Your honest review will help me grow as a writer and motivate me to create more engaging stories in the future.

Thank you once again for taking the time to explore my book. I genuinely hope it proved to be a rewarding experience for you. Your support means everything to me, and I am truly grateful to each reader who joins me on this journey. Together, we can cultivate a vibrant community of readers and writers united by our love for storytelling.

Each review contributes to a vibrant dialogue that enriches our literary experience. I look forward to hearing your thoughts and insights as we continue to explore the depths of creativity together. Your feedback is invaluable, and it inspires me to keep pushing the boundaries of my writing. Let's keep the conversation going and delve deeper into the stories that connect us all.

Dr Andrew C S Koh

Scan the QR code below to discover more

Scan the QR code below to download a review copy of Walking in His Footsteps.

Scan QR Code below to discover

From Darkness to Light

I wandered long in shadows deep,
A heart weighed down, no peace to keep.
Lost in the world, without a guide,
No steady place where I could hide.

But in the midst of storm and strife,
I heard a call, a voice of life.
It whispered hope, it spoke of grace,

Of mercy flowing from a Savior's face.

I turned to Him with all my pain,
He washed me clean, removed the stain.
The chains that bound me fell away,

And in His arms, I chose to stay.

Now every step is led by Him,
Through valleys dark or waters dim.
I walk in faith, no longer bound,
For in His love, my joy is found.

From darkness into light I've come,

A child redeemed, a wanderer home.

And with each breath, I now proclaim,
The mighty power of Jesus' name.

www.drandrewcskoh.com/poems

Don't miss out!

Visit the website below and you can sign up to receive emails whenever Dr Andrew C S Koh publishes a new book. There's no charge and no obligation.

https://books2read.com/r/B-A-FMXV-SGMDF

BOOKS 2 READ

Connecting independent readers to independent writers.

Did you love *Walking in His Footsteps: A Pilgrim's Journey*? Then you should read *From Stethoscope to Wisdom*[1] by Dr Andrew C S Koh!

[2]

From Healing Hands to Divine Wisdom.

From Stethoscope to Wisdom explores the intersection of medicine, faith, and personal growth. Dr. Andrew C. S. Koh, blending his experience as a doctor with profound spiritual insights, offers a transformative journey toward deeper wisdom and purpose. A compelling read for those seeking holistic healing in mind, body, and spirit.

From Stethoscope to Wisdom delves into the powerful convergence of medicine, faith, and personal development. The author skillfully combines medical knowledge with deep spiritual insights, leading readers on a transformative journey to greater wisdom and

---

1. https://books2read.com/u/3nPEVK

2. https://books2read.com/u/3nPEVK

purpose. This book is a captivating read for anyone seeking holistic healing for their mind, body, and spirit—a true must-read!

Read more at https://www.drandrewcskoh.com.

Also by Dr Andrew C S Koh

Bible Study
From Creation to Covenant
From Deceiver to Destiny: Jacob's Story
From Slavery to Freedom
From Man to Mission
From Slave to Brother
From Symbols to Salvation
From Legalism to Liberty
From Tribulation to Triumph

Daily Devotion
Manna of Life: Daily Devotion

Daily Devotions
Bread of Life Daily Devotions
Words of Eternal Life
Bread From Heaven: Daily Devotions
Light of the World Daily Devotions
Light of the World Daily Devotions
The Way, the Truth, and the Life

Rooted: A Daily Devotion to Deepen your Faith

Fiction
The Hourglass Paradox

Genesis
Understanding Genesis 1-11: From Adam to Abraham
Faith Journey of Abraham: Genesis 12-25
Life Story of Jacob: Genesis 26-36
The Story of Joseph: Genesis 37-50
From Pit to Palace

Gospels and Act
The Gospel According to Matthew
Daily Devotion Gospel of Mark
The Gospel According to Luke
Daily Devotion Gospel of John
Acts: Volume 1 and 2, From Jerusalem to Rome
From Galilee to Golgotha

Non Pauline and General Epistles
Hebrews: the Just Shall Live by Faith
1 John, 2 John, 3 John & Jude: a Verse by Verse Bible Study
General Epistles: 1 Peter, 2 Peter, James

Pauline Epistles
Romans: The Just Shall Live by Faith
1 Corinthians
2 Corinthians
1 Thessalonians, 2 Thessalonians, Philemon
Pastoral Epistles: 1 Timothy, 2 Timothy, Titus
Galatians: Justified by Faith in Jesus Christ
Philemon: Charge to the Master's Account

Prison Epistles
The Prison Epistles
Philippians: Rejoice Always in the Lord
Colossians: He is the Image of the Invisible God
Ephesians: Every Spiritual Blessings

Reflective Poems
Journey in Ryhme: Poems of Reflection
Whispers of Grace

Standalone
Apocalypse: Understanding the Book of Revelation
Expository Preaching
Memoirs of a Doctor
Moses: Let My People Go
Living Word Living Savior
From Stethoscope to Wisdom

Walking in His Footsteps: A Pilgrim's Journey
Mapping the Heart
The Forgotten Melody
Footprints in Time
From Love to Light
Time Traveller's Return
The hourglass Paradox

Watch for more at https://www.drandrewcskoh.com.

About the Author

Dr Andrew C S Koh a retired cardiologist, Bible teacher, and author of 50 titles. With a passion for making Scripture come alive, he blends theological insight with practical life application to help readers grow in faith and understanding. His writing reflects a deep commitment to God's Word, forged through decades of medical service, spiritual study, and personal devotion. Dr. Koh's works have encouraged believers around the world to walk closer with Christ and live out their calling with purpose and conviction.

Koh's unique perspective blends his extensive knowledge of the medical field with his deep theological insights. He studied theology at Laidlaw College in Auckland, New Zealand. He now calls Malaysia home, where he lives with his family. He made history in 2021 by setting a record in the Malaysia Book of Records for publishing the most books in a single year.

Whether he's teaching the Bible, creating digital content, or sharing his thoughts through various media, Dr. Koh's mission is clear: to make the Word of God accessible and relevant to everyday life. His works aim to inspire believers to grow deeper in their faith, live with purpose, and embrace the transformative power of God's love.

Link tree:

https://linktr.ee/andrewcskoh

https://books.drandrewcskoh.com/link-tree

free ebook:

https://storyoriginapp.com/giveaways/b295be58-7736-11ec-ac4b-e34d930c508e

Read more at https://www.drandrewcskoh.com.

About the Publisher

At *Dr. Andrew C. S. Koh Publishing*, we are dedicated to publishing Christ-centered, Scripture-based resources that edify the church, equip believers, and spread the gospel. Our aim is to glorify God by helping readers grow in biblical knowledge, spiritual maturity, and faithful living.

Rooted in Scripture and committed to the Great Commission, we exist to proclaim the timeless truths of God's Word through books, Bible studies, and resources for spiritual growth.

Whether you're a seeker, student, or seasoned believer, our mission is to help you deepen your faith and walk in the light of Christ.

Read more at https://www.drandrewcskoh.com.